Reprogramming Your Money-Mind

Wendy Aridela

Copyright © 2016 Wendy Aridela

All rights reserved.

ISBN-13: 978-1539098249

ISBN-10: 1539098249

Contents

INTRODUCTION 2
  Are your Money-Programs scrambled? 2
  How to use this book 3
DISCLAIMER 5
SECTION ONE - Reprogramming the mental level 7
  What this Section is About 7
  What are beliefs? 9
  Why are beliefs important? 11
  How do beliefs shape our reality? 13
  Where do our beliefs come from? 14
Your Beliefs About The World 17
  Recognising your limiting beliefs 17
  Questionnaire 1 20
  Questionnaire 2 22
  Questionnaire 3 25
Creative Thinking - the Riches Between Your Ears . 30
  The truth about Divine help 33
Solving the World's Problems 34
  Your Special Training Curriculum 34
  How to Play the Google Game 36
Clarity - the Importance of Knowing What You Want
.... 39

Breaking the Cycle..42
Becoming aware of what you're doing 42
Becoming Clear About What You Want Instead...43
Scene 2 - The New Program 46
Using Both Sides of Your Brain..............................50
Left Brain - Making Action Plans 51
Left Brain - Planning SMART 54
Left Brain - Scheduling.....................................57
Right Brain - Working with the Big Picture 58
Right Brain - Sleep on It!..................................62
SECTION TWO - Reprogramming the spiritual level 65
What this section is about 65
You Are God's Adventure..66
Health Warning! 66
Why the heck are you here? 67
How I came up with such a mad idea 68
Why pick a life of challenges? 74
Becoming who you are...78
Your Reflection in the World..............................80
Focusing on Breathing.......................................82
How good are you at receiving? 83
Being open to opportunities 84
Money as a Spiritual Practice 86
The Law of Attraction - the Simple Version 89

Reprogramming your Money-Mind

- The Law of Attraction for Grown-Ups 92
- Opening to Guidance 100
  - How does intuition work? 100
  - How do I turn it on? 100
  - Ways to work with intuition 101
  - Working with Guides 102
  - Asking your Higher Self for guidance 104
  - The legacy of ancestral beliefs 106
- SECTION THREE - Reprogramming the emotional level 110
  - What this section is about 110
- Discovering Your Values 111
  - The Values cards 112
  - Some questions to ask yourself 118
- The Value of Generosity 120
  - Working with Jealousy and Envy 122
  - Stopping Complaining 123
  - Working with Wanting 125
- Forgiveness - the big step forwards 128
  - Releasing the pain of the past 131
  - After forgiveness, what then? 134
- Letting Go of Stress 136
  - Putting yourself in the driver's seat 137
  - Dealing with Fear 140

Fear and family stories 140

Fear of loss, lack and going without 141

How to cope with Fear - practical strategies 145

Mastering your mood - how to feel good more of the time 149

Laughing and Smiling - your secret weapons ... 149

Roaring and Groaning - releasing anger and frustration 152

Meditation - the Secret of Calm 153

SECTION FOUR - Reprogramming the physical level 158

What this Section is About 158

Getting Real with your money 160

Real like a rich person (really!) 160

Fearless Finances 162

Where are you? Tracking the money-flow 163

Your financial plan 165

Increasing Your Income 169

Your Skills Audit 170

Turning your expertise into money 174

Having a business "on the side" 180

Network Marketing 180

Saving - Your super-highway to wealth 183

I can't afford to save 183

Feeling good about saving 186
Making saving more rewarding 189
Savings Accounts - which ones would feel best for you? 190
Investing - creating a better world for your children 195
What kind of world do you want? 196
Set Yourself Up for Success! 198
Clutter-clearing - making way for new opportunities 198
The Feng Shui 'Magic' 200
Letting go of the past 201
Your appearance 202
Don't stop with your clothes - change your body, too! 204
Finding the way through 209
The 'Richard Branson' exercise 209
Getting help 211
CONCLUSION: what are the changes you want to see? 215
EXTRA BITS 219
My Story 219
FREE REPORT – THE 7 Mistakes that shut the door to Abundance 224
More Books by Wendy Aridela 225

Living at the Crossroads 225
The Goddesses of Abundance 226
How to Meditate 227

Introduction
What's Wrong with my Money Programming?

INTRODUCTION

Are your Money-Programs scrambled?

Do you:

- worry about money?
- wake up feeling stressed about money?
- spend far too much of your time making it at a job you don't like, but can't leave (because of the money)?
- never seem to save it?
- know your spending is out of control?
- feel you can't easily allow yourself to spend it?
- work so many hours to get your money that you don't have enough time for hobbies or to spend with the people you care about - or even to sleep?
- feel embarrassed, ashamed, guilty or insecure if the conversation turns to money?
- feel that how much money you make somehow defines what you're worth as a person?
- never seem to quite have enough - whenever more money comes in, so do unexpected expenses?
- live in constant debt that doesn't seem to get less?
- feel that money is the biggest problem in your life?
- feel that all the other problems in your life would go away if you only had enough money?

Reprogramming your Money-Mind

Did you answer **yes**? To even one or two? Then your money-programming is scrambled and you need to reprogram your Money-Mind.

This book will help you to work out where you're getting stuck and sabotaging yourself. It will help you find ways to earn more, attract more and save more as well as to feel better around the money you have. As you read it, you'll begin to see how you can have a saner relationship with money, one in which making money is a balanced part of a happier and more fulfilling life.

Let's get started!

How to use this book

Obviously, you are one whole person - you are not divided into four separate levels, labelled Mental, Spiritual, Emotional and Physical. But, for the purposes of discovering the glitches and gremlins in your Money-Programming, it's useful to separate out the different kinds of ways you might be blocking yourself.

This is because most people are not equally blocked on every level. You might have an excellent job with a high salary, for example, but find that you never seem to be able to reach the next level. Or find that, no matter how much you earn, you can never seem to save. So your blocks don't seem to be on the physical level, but are probably tied up with some of your beliefs around money.

Or you may be one of the people who feel drawn to earn their living from healing or offering spiritual counselling. You know your work is good and that, at your best, you are a channel for Spirit to act through you - but you barely earn enough to live on. Your spiritual level obviously has a clear and open connection, but you may lack some straightforward money-making skills on the physical level or have some limiting beliefs about money and spirituality.

Money-Program glitches tends to be complex and multi-levelled. Most of us have blocks on more than one level. So, the easiest way to use this book is to read it straight through, picking and choosing the ideas and strategies on each level that seem to resonate with you most clearly.

If you feel that you already have a clear understanding about where your biggest blocks are or have a particular issue you'd like to work on first, simply turn to the relevant section and start there. The sections are fairly independent of each other, so you can skip sections or flip back and forth, just reading the bits that seem relevant and useful to you at any given time.

This book is based on my own experience, so some of the ideas and suggestions I put forward may not work for you. I'm not any kind of guru or ultimate authority, so do feel free to discard the bits the don't work for you and to focus on the bits that do!

DISCLAIMER

This book is based on my own experiences. I'm not a Financial Advisor, an Accountant or a debt counsellor. Nothing in here is meant to replace the advice of qualified professionals.

Seek qualified advice before making decisions about investments, savings or debt management.

Section 1
Reprogramming the Mental Level

SECTION ONE - Reprogramming the mental level

What this Section is About

Many people will find that some of their biggest blocks to allowing a greater, smoother flow of money into their life are right between their ears! So this section explains how you can set about discovering and replacing your limiting beliefs around money.

Maybe you don't think you have limiting or disempowering beliefs around money? You'd be in one of the smallest minorities in the developed world if you didn't have. Crazy, limiting and disempowering beliefs about money are built into the very foundations of our societies - to such an extent that most of us don't even see these ideas as beliefs. We think that this is the way things *are*. Many of us can't even begin to imagine that there could be other ways of thinking about things.

Worse still, many of our beliefs about money, about rich people, about poor people, about life and work and ourselves, are totally unconscious. We often don't even know that we hold particular beliefs until something arises to contradict them or to make us question ourselves.

You can't change anything you're not aware of - so this section helps you to become more aware of just

Wendy Aridela

what is lying inside your head - pun intended! Let's start by looking at why beliefs are so important.

Beliefs - and how they shape your world.

What are beliefs?

Your beliefs can provide some of the biggest blocks to becoming all you can be, having a sizeable increase in income or becoming more successful in any way that seems valuable or relevant to you. So why is this?

First of all, let's look at what a belief is. One way of looking at it is that a belief is a pattern of thinking, a repeated story that you tell yourself, backed up with a certain emotional tone that - for you - signals "Yes, this is true." Both the pattern of thinking and the emotional tone are important.

The pattern of thinking helps you to make sense of the world. Let's suppose that you have a belief that says "Boy Scouts are particularly helpful and public spirited young people." One day, you see a young man helping an elderly person carry their shopping onto the bus. The thought may cross your mind, "What a helpful lad - I expect he's been a Boy Scout." You fit what you see into your belief system.

On the other hand, suppose you see some boys wearing Boy Scout uniform pushing in front of a queue to get onto a train. This is contrary to your belief system. What you'll probably do is to make up an explanation. "Those boys must only have been in the Boy Scouts for a very short time - they've forgotten their manners." Or even, "I don't expect to see behaviour like that from Boy Scouts - those boys must be an exception." If you have a strong belief, it will take some powerful evidence to the contrary to shift it. Instead, you'll tend to discount anything you see as an exception to your rule or as a one-off oddity.

The emotional tone is important, too, because it's your internal "convincer" signal. How do you know if something is true? You just *do*. There's a feeling to it. You know this from times when you have tried to convince yourself of something you can't quite believe. You can maybe see the sense in the words, but it just doesn't *feel* true for you.

This can be a problem with some people when they try using affirmations. They've read that this is a very powerful way to create change in their lives, and so they are all enthusiastic about the idea. They stand in front of a mirror, looking into the eyes of their reflection and saying something like, "I am a wonderful person. I deserve to be rich."

The words are wonderful. They *want* to believe them. But no matter how often they repeat the words, there is something inside that is not convinced. That 'convincer' feeling tone is just not there. So our affirmation-users stand there, repeating their affirmations in as sincere a tone of voice as they can manage, while all the time, there's this little voice inside repeating, "Fake! Fake! Fake!"

Why are beliefs important?

This leads very smoothly and easily into an understanding of why your beliefs are so important. They determine the world you experience, to a large extent. In fact, if something is too much against your belief system you may never see it at all - you will simply delete it from conscious awareness. Let me give you an example to show how that works.

Suppose you come to believe that your boss thinks you are stupid. You may not even be consciously aware of why you think that - you just *know*. What is probably going on, is that every time your boss seems irritated when you speak to her, you register the irritation and explain it with your belief-story. "My boss is irritated with me because I'm making a mess of explaining this and now she thinks I'm even more of an idiot." In fact, your boss may have a headache, or have come to work after a row over the breakfast table with her teenage son. Her irritation may be nothing to do with you!

But not only are you choosing to interpret her behaviour in a particular way, you have quite possibly now created a self-fulfilling prophecy. Because you believe that your boss thinks you're an idiot, you're very nervous around her and lacking in confidence. So, when she looks up with that world-weary expression on her face as you approach her, you drop all your papers on the floor from nervousness. You now have to waste several minutes of her time while you pick everything up again and get your papers into the right order. By now, she probably *is* irritated with you and *does* think you are being a bit of an idiot! Can you see? You have just created the very thing you were afraid of.

Not only that, but because of your belief, you are always on the look-out for behaviour on her part that might indicate she is getting annoyed with you. So you notice every frown, every sigh, every time she rolls her eyes heaven-wards as you approach. You tend to talk to her as if you expect her to bite. You're hyper-alert for danger signals the whole time even when, in reality, there is no danger there. Your boss is going to react to that - probably by finding you rather annoying to be around. Why are you always so afraid of her? she may think. You must be an idiot!

At the same time, you are deleting every time she looks around the office with a contented gaze. You don't even register the times she smiles at you. If she asks you how you are, in a pleasant way, you may be wondering where the catch is. What does she want to spring on you now? Is she looking for evidence that you're under stress? Does she want to fire you? Even though your boss is trying to be nice to you, your beliefs change everything you see connected with her into some degree of threat. You cannot believe that she likes you or respects you. And so, over time, you're likely to make your beliefs come true.

How do beliefs shape our reality?

How is this happening in the brain? Psychologists have estimated that our conscious minds are only capable of handling around 7 pieces of information at once. However, our unconscious minds are handling maybe 11 million bits of data per second. Right now, your subconscious mind is monitoring the blood circulation in your toes. It knows how tense your shoulder muscles are. It's paying constant attention to all the background sounds you haven't been aware of (until you read this - did you start noticing them just now?) All the time, it's scanning inside your body and all around you, checking that everything is OK.

If we became aware of all of this information consciously, we'd go into complete overload. So, deep in our brains we have a filtering mechanism called the reticular activating system (which I'm going to abbreviate to RAS from now on.)The job of the RAS is to decide which 7 of the 11 million bits of information to bring to your conscious awareness. Priority number one is to keep you safe, so anything that could be a threat comes through loud and clear. If there's nothing immediately threatening, it makes its choice in the same way as online shops like Amazon work:

"If you like that, you may well be interested in this."
"Other people who browsed those things also bought these things."

In other words, your RAS looks through the logs of your previous behaviour to see what's most likely to be relevant. So, knowing that you have an emotional response every time your boss has a particular facial expression, or uses a certain tone of voice, those aspects of your boss must be important to you. Therefore, it will show you more of them. "Watch out, she's rearranging her facial features - is this a frown coming on? Yes, yes! Look, she's seen you watching her and now she's frowning. That's because she thinks you're a moron."

On the other hand, your RAS won't bother to alert you if your boss is smiling because you've never shown any interest before in boss-smiling-behaviour. There's a saying, "I'll believe it when I see it." But can you see that, in reality, things work the other way around? You see it *because* you believe it!

Where do our beliefs come from?

What this means is that your beliefs are constantly shaping your reality in a way which isn't under your conscious control. You see the reality you expect to see. You almost constantly have the experience of your beliefs turning out to be true. Now this would be tricky enough if, when you were 18, you'd had a special day when you sat down with a wise counsellor and chose all the beliefs that would run your life from now on. But - as we all know - life isn't like that.

Most of us have a complete rag-bag of assorted beliefs that we've picked up from all over the place. We get them from our parents, from school, from religious teachings (even if you're not religious, you pick stuff up!) We get them from the television, from newspapers and from the Internet. We adopt some of our friends' beliefs. We get stuff from books, films, and videos. We even pick up beliefs from advertisements. (I would bet money that almost all of what most people think they know about cholesterol has come from advertisements for margarine!)

We don't choose our beliefs at all - in fact, it doesn't even occur to us most of the time that these thoughts, these stories-for-making-sense-of-the-world that we have are simply beliefs. To us, they are the truth. That's how the world is. And we can *prove* it, because look - the world behaves just as we believe it will. So this story-for-making-sense, this pattern that I am applying to my life is not just a belief. It's not just a habitual pattern of thinking. It's the real, genuine, as-it-is description of Reality. Except it isn't.

Obviously, that's not to say that everything we believe in isn't true. Of course not. There is a general agreement among most of the people on the planet that the sky is blue and that water is wet. You're not just making it up. There is a broad area of consensus. But the difficulty comes with more personal beliefs such as what you believe about yourself, what you believe about your family, about money, success, rich people, poor people, how to be spiritual, and what you should be doing with your life. These are the beliefs that act like negative programming, beliefs that can get in your way and sabotage your success.

Reprogramming your Money-Mind

Your Beliefs About The World

Let's take a closer look at the beliefs that interfere most powerfully with our abilities to become all that we are. These include our beliefs about what kind of a person we are, what we can do and what we can't do, what people think about us and whether - or how much - that matters. They also include our beliefs about what money is, how important it is, and what "the rules" are for getting it. We are also likely to have limiting beliefs about the economy, success, being rich, being poor, being spiritual, being visible, being a worthwhile and valuable person, how people make a difference in the world and the degree to which it's even possible for us to make a difference. Many of us may also doubt the value of our gifts, skills and expertise and how much anyone would be willing to pay us for it. The list goes on - you can probably add some more unhelpful beliefs of your own!

Recognising your limiting beliefs

These thinking programs - because that's all beliefs are - can be very undermining, causing us to act small and to live much smaller lives than we could be doing. Worse still, these are often some of the beliefs that we don't recognise *as beliefs*. We think this is the way the world is. After all, many of these beliefs have been drummed into us from childhood, often coming from Mum and Dad and Grandma and our teachers - people we respect and believe. If we were repeatedly told things such as "Money doesn't grow on trees - we can't afford that," or "Who do you think you are? - nobody wants to hear what you've got to say," then, to us, these are often absorbed as truths in the same way as we believe "The grass is green," or "Daddy is a man and Mummy is a woman." After all, our parents and teachers believed what they told us and acted out their beliefs in their own lives.

So, if we constantly got told by our parents that money was in short supply, it's likely this was backed up by a lot of evidence to show us that this was true. We probably caught Mum and Dad having worried conversations about a bigger than expected bill that had turned up. We saw Mum pick up items in shops, read the price labels and then reluctantly put them back and choose a cheaper alternative. We ate meals made from last night's leftovers or had shepherd's pie for several nights in a row because the butcher was selling lamb mince on special offer for a bulk buy. We could see that it was true that money really *was* in short supply.

I'm certainly not trying to persuade you that your memories of childhood are somehow delusional and that actually, you grew up in the lap of luxury! But can you see that the past does not equal the future? Your parents and teachers believed whatever they believed, and lived lives that were an honest reflection of their beliefs. *But you can choose to live differently.*

Have you heard the saying, "If you keep on doing what you're doing, you'll keep on getting what you're getting?" It's generally true - but what happens if you choose to do something different? What happens if you stop doing things the way you've always done them, stop believing that life has to be the way it's always been and stop hiding your light under a bushel from the mistaken belief that nobody wants to look at it, anyway? Your life changes, that's what.

But you can only change what you are conscious of. You can't change belief patterns if you're still seeing them as the Ultimate Truth about how the world is. To be able to change a belief, you have to recognise:

- that it is a belief, not The Truth
- that it isn't serving you and
- that you want to change it.

Finally, you have to replace it with a new, more useful and empowering belief - you can't just leave a gap in your head!

So, how do you spot those limiting beliefs? Below, you'll find some questionnaires that ask you to think through what you believe about various things. Take them seriously and put some real thought into them. Don't just write down the answers you think are the "right" ones. Take time to tune in and to ask yourself what you truly believe on a deep level. For example, you may have been brought up to believe that it was selfish, shallow and materialistic to want expensive things. But when you are really honest with yourself you can maybe see that you would actually quite like a luxury car, or a beautiful home by the sea - it's just that you usually push such thoughts out of awareness whenever they arise, or cover them up by indignation at "rich people who drive round in flash cars," or "posh people who live in million-pound mansions."

It's worth writing down even the things you don't think are beliefs at all - the things you genuinely think are facts. For example, "money is real." Sometimes, these are the very things that make light-bulbs turn on in your head, because, once you see them written down, you can see that they could just be a belief and may not be true, after all!

Questionnaire 1

What do you think about rich people?

Finish the statement "Rich people are....." in as many ways as you can. Try to complete 20. This may not be easy but keep going. It's often the definitions you come up with after the first few easy answers that generate the most insight for you.

Reprogramming your Money-Mind

Rich people are………	
1	
2	
3	
4	
5	
6	
7	
8	
9	
10	
11	
12	
13	
14	

15	
16	
17	
18	
19	
20	

If you don't want to mark your book, you can download a copy of this questionnaire here:

http://ow.ly/Uessl

Questionnaire 2

What do you think about money?

Take a few minutes to read each belief and to let it sink in so you are responding more from the heart than the surface. Give each statement a mark from 1-10 where 1= I totally disagree with this and 10 = Absolutely! I couldn't agree more!

Reprogramming your Money-Mind

Statement	Mark
The rich get richer and the poor get poorer.	8
Greed is one of the Seven Deadly Sins - for a good reason.	0
Money is the root of all evil.	0
Money is a form of Divine Energy.	10
We live in a totally abundant Universe.	10
It's better to give than to receive.	6
Money is simply a convenient form of exchange.	8
Money is a way of judging how successful people are.	10
It's difficult to be both wealthy and spiritual.	10
Wealthy people can do more good in the world than poor people.	6
There is a limited amount of money - so not everyone could be rich.	0

Wendy Aridela

Money can't buy happiness.	5
The best things in life are free.	8
The more you have, the more you are able to give.	9
There's absolutely nothing wrong with spending money on nice things and luxuries - if I earn a lot of money, it's up to me what I spend it on.	8
A lot of poor people stay poor because they have no intention to work or to contribute to society.	6
Money should be shared out fairly - it's ridiculous that the top 1% of wealthy people own as much as the next 90% put together.	8
Money is just a way for politicians and bankers to manipulate people.	8
I would like to have a lot more money.	10
It's only fair that people get well repaid for their skills, talents and expertise.	10
Money is the root of most of the fear that holds me back.	10

Reprogramming your Money-Mind

The idea that being poor and being spiritual go together is an idea long past its sell-by date.	10
The way to make more money is to start thinking and acting like a wealthy person.	10
I value money.	5

Questionnaire 3

What do you think about success?

Take a few minutes to read each belief and to let it sink in so you are responding more from the heart than the surface. Give each statement a mark from 1-10 where 1= I totally disagree with this and 10 = Absolutely! I couldn't agree more!

Statement	Mark
I consider myself to be successful.	
For me, other things are much more important than money in deciding how successful I am.	

Wendy Aridela

For me, the ability to make a difference in the world is the biggest measure of success.
To be successful, you have to be rich.
Things like luxury cars and designer clothes show people how successful you are.
Real success is spiritual - it's about becoming more of who you really are.
You look at a person with a Rolls-Royce and an 8-bedroom house and you can't help seeing them as successful.
Success, for me, is linked to how creative I can be.
Once you realise that the greatest money-making capacity you have lies between your ears, there's no limit to how successful you can be.
Anyone can be successful - they just have to want it enough.
For me, success is about winning.

Reprogramming your Money-Mind

I think a truly successful life is one where lots of people will be genuinely sad when you die.	
For me, real success is linking up with something bigger than yourself and devoting your energy to it - whether that's your country, your church, your planet, a charity or even just your family.	
If you haven't achieved success by age 40, well, it's not going to happen, is it?	
For me, success is all about the freedom to make my own rules.	
A successful person is someone with happy children who grow up to be good people, contributing to society and respecting and loving their parents.	
I think success is all about making God smile.	
For me, success is about creating and cultivating beauty.	
Success can be measured by the number of your friends.	

Wendy Aridela

> Success happens when you set out to do something and you achieve it.

This is obviously not a comprehensive list! It's simply designed to get you thinking and maybe to give you some AHA! moments of insight. Once you start thinking about issues such as these, you probably start to see that a lot of the simple, obvious answers become much more foggy and unclear when you give them some thought.

But even from these few simple exercises, it's easy to understand that your beliefs can be like quicksand. You've probably already discovered that several of your beliefs contradict each other - most people do!

Also, as you start the process of becoming more consciously aware of what you *do* believe, it's sometimes easy to see where your beliefs have been tripping you up in life. How many of your beliefs are helpful, empowering and supportive? How many are undermining and discouraging? Can you see that your beliefs could have been affecting you for years, acting below the surface to limit your opportunities, your success and your achievements?

The good news is, that simply by becoming aware of your beliefs and recognising them as limitations, you have done maybe 80% of the work necessary to change them. The next step is to start empowering yourself by choosing some replacement beliefs that are more positive and more consistent. I'll be showing you some ways to do that later in the book.

Wendy Aridela

Creative Thinking - the Riches Between Your Ears

There's a joke that you may have heard before:

In a village not far from here, there was once a terrible flood. The river burst its banks and the water level began to rise until soon it was flooding the houses. All the villagers started preparing to evacuate. They packed their belongings into cars and set off for higher ground.

On the way, two villagers passed the church where the pastor was standing on the doorstep, apparently praying with outstretched arms.

"Would you like a lift, pastor?" the villagers asked. "We have room enough in our car for one more." "Thank you kindly," replied the pastor, "but it's all right. God has promised to save me."

The villagers looked doubtful, for the water was rising very fast, but who were they to question the faith of a holy man? So they drove on, and the water continued to rise.

Soon, it was so deep that the roads were impassable and the few remaining villagers were escaping in boats. As they rowed through the flooded streets and over the flooded gardens, they passed the church, where the pastor was now kneeling on the roof, deep in prayer.

Reprogramming your Money-Mind

"Hey, Pastor," the villagers shouted, "Come on down and get into our boat. We can fit in one more and the water is only a few inches below the church roof now. You'll surely drown if you stay there."
"You're very good," replied the pastor, "and I thank you very kindly. But don't worry about me, for God has promised to save me."

The villagers shrugged - who were they to question the faith of a holy man to whom God had promised personal rescue? But the waters were now swirling dangerously and the currents were strong, so they didn't want to spend time arguing. Smiling politely, they rowed away.

Just before nightfall, the Army finally sent out a search-and-rescue helicopter to round up any stray survivors. The helicopter crew spotted the pastor clinging to the church steeple and shouted down to him through a bull-horn:
"Don't you worry, sir - we're sending down a crew-man on a ladder!"
They dropped the ladder down and a crew-man descended.

"Lucky we came by when we did, sir," the crew-man said with a broad smile.
"We got here in the nick of time, I'd say. The water is already up to your knees. I'd say you were less than an hour away from certain death. Come on

now, sir, and hold onto me, while I haul you to safety."
"That's really most kind of you," replied the pastor, "and believe me, I appreciate your effort. But you don't have to rescue me because I have God's assurance that He will save me." And to the crew-man's astonishment, he refused to let go of the steeple and climb the ladder.

Well, what can you do? The crew-man was hanging on a ladder below a hovering helicopter, over swirling waters and it was getting dark. It was much too dangerous to try to wrestle the pastor off the steeple and up the ladder, so, reluctantly, he climbed the ladder and the helicopter flew away.

20 minutes later, the pastor drowned, and arrived at the pearly gates of Heaven in something of a temper.
"God, my Father and Saviour," the pastor shouted, "What were you playing at? You **promised** me! You promised me that you would save me and then you let me drown!"
"My child," came the booming voice of God, " I sent you a car, a boat and a helicopter - What more did you want?"

Reprogramming your Money-Mind

The truth about Divine help

The story is somewhat silly, but it makes a useful point. Divine help doesn't always look like a band of angels turning up at our door. It's more likely to look like something utterly ordinary and mundane - a boat or a car, for example. We may pray for help with money problems - and fail to recognise the help when it arrives because it doesn't look like money. It may look like a job advertisement in the paper. Or like this book!

It could even look like a bright idea that we wake up with one morning. That happened to Robert Louis Stevenson, who woke up with the whole story of "Treasure Island" in his head one day. He wrote it down and it became one of the most famous children's books of all time.

There's another story that's relevant here - this time, about a man who met up with a Saint.

"Why does God let bad things happen?" asked the man. "Doesn't He care about the world? There's starvation and war, pollution and poverty, cruelty and ugliness everywhere - and yet God does nothing! Why doesn't He do something to help?"

*"My brother," replied the Saint, "The last time I looked at the figures, God had placed on this planet 7 **billion** solutions to the world's problems. Which problem are **you** the solution to?"*

Wendy Aridela

Solving the World's Problems

Every single problem has a solution. Bright ideas are all around. Have you ever noticed how sometimes, similar scientific discoveries happen at about the same time, in places thousands of miles apart? Or people at opposite sides of the globe will come up with almost identical inventions? It's as if the ideas are floating in the atmosphere, just waiting for someone to ask the right questions.

In the same way that God in the story acted to rescue the pastor through other people, that's the way God acts to solve the world's problems, too. The solutions are out there and they come into being through people. People get bright ideas, act to make them work and one more problem gets solved.

Maybe there's a solution waiting for you to find? Maybe there's something you can do to help the world? In fact, I can guarantee it! It doesn't have to be something dramatic like finding the solution to world poverty or war. Your solution might be to help find homes for abandoned animals, to help little children learn to read, to cook great food or to provide cheerful and efficient service in a shop or restaurant.

Your Special Training Curriculum

Looking back on your life, it might look like a disorderly jumble. You might have had all kinds of odd life experiences. Your CV might look like a cut-and-paste job from 3 or 4 entirely different people. You may have gone through some really tough times. But what if it wasn't all an accident? What if it wasn't random? What if your life was a special training programme - a special curriculum, designed for you, personally? What has it trained you for? What can you now do in a way that's different from anyone else? What problem have you come through in a way that enables you to help others going through something similar? Where have you got skills or knowledge from totally different fields that you can put together to create something that's never been done before?

Many of the world's greatest scientific discoveries have been made by scientists who were trained in one discipline and then swapped fields so were able to apply the thinking from one field to the problems of another. James Watt invented the steam engine after paying attention to the way a boiling kettle generated enough force to rattle its own lid. James Dyson invented the Dyson dual cyclone vacuum cleaner after seeing an extractor fan in a paint factory. You are no less creative than these men. Your greatest wealth is likely to lie between your ears, in the creative thinking capacity of your brain. Where have you got experiences from one area that could provide new solutions in another area? To find out, you could try playing "The Google Game."

Wendy Aridela

How to Play the Google Game

Think of two areas of your life where you have skills, knowledge, interest or expertise. This gets more interesting the more different the two areas are. For example, for myself, I Googled "steam trains + knitting." Yours could be "dog care + crochet" or "organic gardening+ nuclear physics." You get the idea, I'm sure. What you'll now discover are some astonishing ideas for how to combine those unlikely skills - that could potentially enable you to earn a living from them.

For my own example, I discovered someone with a business creating knitting patterns for replica steam-trains which could be used as bolster cushions in a den or study, or simply as decorations. I also discovered companies that specialise in steam-train holiday packages for knitting enthusiasts. Look it up! Try several different pairings of your skills, talents and interests and be prepared to be inspired!

Some of the ideas you come up with won't appeal to you at all. But who knows? You may get inspiration for something completely new. Or you could read about someone who has combined two of your skills and interests and realise that what has worked for them could work for you, too. That product or service could be just what your neighbourhood wants. If you're not sure, ask to be shown 3 times and then watch out for a similar idea or something linked to it, getting mentioned by a friend, or on TV, or in a book or on an advertisement ..... If it's meant for you, the Universe can make it very clear!

We've all heard of people who lived ordinary lives until some crisis came along. All of a sudden, their lives changed direction. What seemed at first to be a catastrophe, or a serious problem turned out to be a blessing in disguise because it forced that person to open up to inspiration, try something new, take a different path. What if your scrambled money-programming is **your** blessing in disguise? What if it's God's invitation to you to open up to something entirely unexpected, some new opportunity that you would never have thought of or even considered before?

Abundance is a two-way street, after all. When we think of having more abundance in our lives it's easy to focus on money coming in. But what is going out, from us, is equally important. We all have a gift to give. This is not a Universe with spare parts. Everyone has a role to play. Maybe this crisis is a way of opening you up to be a channel for Divine creativity and problem-solving to flow through you to make a difference in the world. This will then create a flow back to you of Divine energy, in the forms of money, satisfaction, the praise and thanks of the people you help - and yet more creative ideas.

Wendy Aridela

All you need to do is to ask - and then to stay open to creative ideas and to act on them!

Clarity - the Importance of Knowing What You Want

I've already mentioned the role of the Reticular Activating System (RAS) - the part of your brain that chooses which 7 of the 11 million bits of data being processed right now by your subconscious mind your conscious mind is most likely to be interested in. If you remember, its first priority is to alert you to potential threats that might affect your survival. But once it's got any threats out of the way, it chooses what to show you in the same way that online shopping sites such as Amazon do. It looks at what you've shown interest in, in the past, and shows you more of the same.

"You've bought one book by Agatha Christie, so you may be interested in this other book she wrote."

So the RAS will scan through its internal logs of what you have paid attention to and the thoughts you have thought most often and then will scan the environment to find stuff it thinks you will find relevant. So what happens if you've been thinking contradictory things? What if, for example, you've been practising doing affirmations such as:

"Money now comes to me easily and quickly."
"I live in an abundant universe where all my needs are met."
and

Wendy Aridela

"I love money and money loves me?"

Let's imagine you've been sitting doing these affirmations several times a day, for 5-10 minutes each time. So, for maybe half an hour a day, you have been filling your mind with thoughts of wealth and plenty. Let's even imagine that you have managed to do this with a feeling tone of believing what you are saying, at least to some extent. What have you been thinking and saying for the other 23-and-a-half hours every day?

"Oh no! They've taken the payment for the Gas bill out of my account earlier than I expected and now I am short of cash for groceries. I can't believe what bad luck I always have around money!"

"I feel so ill today. But if I take a day off work, I'll get less pay and then we'll be short at the end of the month. My money problems are tiring me out. It's exhausting constantly trying to cope."

" It's one thing after another - I never seem to catch up with my money."

Now then, what do you think your RAS is going to focus on? What is it going to show you more of? Your half-hour of affirmations will definitely have an effect - especially if you have managed to get some positive emotion behind your words. So your RAS might show you a 20p coin that has been dropped on the street for you to pick up, or some money-saving coupons in a magazine. But you have focused so powerfully, and for so much of your day, on worrying about money that - as far as your RAS is concerned - your intentions are quite clear. You feel threatened by information about bills, debts and money problems, so it's really important to alert you to these. So what will you see when you scan through the TV programme guide? The programmes whose titles are going to leap out at you will be things like:

- Can't pay? We'll take it away!
- The Debt Crisis - the dark truth about the economy
- The Problem of Poverty
- Living on Benefits - the war against scroungers

There might be 20 different programmes listed in front of you, but these are the titles that will leap off the page at you. Your RAS will work overtime to keep thoughts of debt and money problems in the forefront of your mind. It's genuinely trying to be helpful - but it ensures that you are living in a tidal wave of information about poverty, debt, money problems and the dire state of the economy. Your world is a pretty dark and gloomy one, at least where money is concerned. Your thoughts and beliefs are creating a vicious circle where you seem to get bigger and bigger servings of the same-old, miserable stuff. This makes it very hard to have the positive outlook that starts finding solutions.

Breaking the Cycle

So how do you break the cycle? This is where the clarity comes in. Firstly, you have to start noticing what you're doing and become aware of your habitual habits of thinking. And secondly, you have to become very clear about what you want instead and to make a conscious decision to stay focused on that. This is simple - but that's not the same as saying that it's easy!

Becoming aware of what you're doing

One way to start noticing your habitual patterns of thinking is to wear one of those rubber bracelets that you can get for donating to a charity. You may have one around the house, or be able to get one for a small donation at a local charity shop. If not, you could use a wide rubber band that fits loosely around your wrist - not too tightly, or you'll restrict your circulation.

Every time you catch yourself worrying about money, or thinking about money in any kind of negative way, swap the bracelet or rubber band to the other wrist. The next time you catch yourself, swap it back again. Keep doing this all day. As well as worries about money, you can include thinking or talking about bills, debts, rent or mortgage payments, or anything else that connects to money and has a feeling tone about it of worry, fear, anxiety, distress, upset, unease or dread.

Reprogramming your Money-Mind

You may be surprised how often you catch yourself swapping that bracelet over! What's more, if you do this for several days, you're likely to find the number of swaps *increasing*. This is not because you're worrying more, but because you're getting much better at noticing the kind of thinking that has normally gone on in the background without much conscious awareness.

Don't mentally beat yourself up when you find yourself worrying. This isn't an exercise to make you feel worse about yourself! Instead, congratulate yourself for becoming aware of your thinking and speaking. As I said before, you can't change anything until you are aware that it's happening. You are taking a giant stride in getting control over your mind and over your life. Congratulations on starting to change your money-programming forever!

Becoming Clear About What You Want Instead

If someone asks you what you want instead of what you've got that can seem like such a ridiculous question, that it's tempting to put on your best Homer Simpson voice and say, "Duh! More money, stupid!" That's such an obvious answer, it's a total no-brainer. But what is "more money?" Does finding 20p on the street count? What about finding £5? Are you thinking of a one-off windfall or of having more money coming in each week? How much more money do you want - realistically? We could all say "Well, I'd like to win the Lotto," but how much money would be enough to make you feel secure?

Do you need an extra £100 each month? An extra £1000? More than that? Would you feel OK on the income you have now, if you could somehow pay off your debts? Could you earn more? Save more? Spend less? Would you be prepared to try? Would you be prepared to do something different, in order to have more money? After all, you know the saying, "If you keep on doing what you've always done, you'll keep on getting what you've always had." So *something* has to change, if you want to have something different. And the place to start is with your thinking.

We've seen already that your RAS will show you more of what you focus upon. This means that, inevitably, there's a lot of the world you simply never see. That's true for everyone, not just you. For example, imagine for a moment being Richard Branson or Bill Gates - someone who is wealthy, influential, and successful. Now imagine that you open the TV Guide. What kinds of programmes do you imagine leap out at people like that? Maybe a documentary about the Far East and the amazing economic opportunities that are opening up there? Perhaps a programme that showcases new inventions? What about a programme on how education is changing as High School children are using more technology and getting lessons about business? You may even have the same programmes or ones like them, featured in your TV Guide, but it's likely you barely noticed them. At the same time, do you think Richard Branson is grabbed by programme titles such as "Can't Pay? We'll Take it Away?" I don't know him, but I would guess not! Why would he be interested in a programme like that?

So what might happen, do you think, if you started focusing on affirmations like this?

"I'm now learning about all kinds of new ways for money to come to me."
"Every day, I am becoming more aware of new opportunities."
"The Universe is now guiding me to find the path to prosperity that is perfect for me."

These affirmations more useful to you than ones such as, "Money now flows into my life in an avalanche of abundance," because they are believable. Affirmations that talk in terms of process are true right now. At this very moment, you almost certainly can't see any avalanches of abundance! But the idea that you are now *learning* to spot new opportunities or that you are *becoming more aware* is credible, even if there don't appear to be any opportunities present right now. You can believe that *the Universe is guiding you right now*, while you are reading this book.

45

Affirmations like this are talking about you and changes happening in you, rather than changes happening in the outside world. You may not have much power over making changes happen in the outside world, but you can certainly control what's happening inside you. These affirmations put the power back in your hands. They tell your RAS to start showing you the opportunities that are all around. (And there are *always* opportunities all around!) They alert you to start noticing all the ways you could be getting guidance - from your intuition, from angels and spiritual helpers, from other people and from quite ordinary and mundane sources such as books and TV programmes.

All of this information has been around you the whole time, but you have barely noticed it. Your RAS has not brought it to your attention, because it didn't think you were interested. But now, it's as if you've loaded a new program onto your internal computer - and all of a sudden, you're getting a completely different output from the same data.

Scene 2 - The New Program

As we've seen, your RAS acts a bit like an internal Google - you give it some keywords and it finds you a whole bunch of information (some of which will be more useful than others!) So, if you get your RAS looking out for "new opportunities" it may come up with some gems, but they are likely to be buried

Reprogramming your Money-Mind

under a pile of fairly useless information. It's like Googling something vague like "Shops" or "Christmas presents." You'll come up with millions of hits but hardly any of them will be what you want. You have to be more specific.

The clearer you are about exactly what you're looking for, the more easily your RAS can find you some good matches. So let's do a bit of day-dreaming. Imagine you wake up tomorrow morning and your kind Fairy Godmother - who you never knew you had - has done a magic spell during the night. All your money problems are now solved! So - what, very specifically, is different? You might come up with a list something like this:

- Instead of owing £7,541 on my credit card, the balance is now £0.
- Instead of having £1.84 in my current account (on only the 16th of the month!) I have £3,250 in there.
- Instead of having £980 coming in at the end of the month, I know I'll be getting £3,750 - and that's every month.
- Instead of being behind with my rent/mortgage payments or my utility bills, everything is now up to date and I have a Direct Debit payment system in place to pay all necessary payments automatically, so I never even have to think about them.

Wendy Aridela

Can you see what I mean? The aim here is to be reasonably sensible. You're not imagining you have won the Lotto or you're a billionaire. You're simply putting some fairly realistic numbers around what you want instead of what you've got. Your numbers may be nothing like my example. You could have much more modest wants or be thinking a whole lot bigger. But my point is that you should come up with something that is believable *for you*. You don't have to have the least idea at this point about the practicalities. You don't have to know how to step up your income from £980 per month to £3750. You don't have to have the foggiest clue about how to pay off that £7,541 on your credit card. But you can be very clear that if you could somehow tick off everything on your list, you'd feel much happier and more secure around money.

What you've just done is to give your RAS some much more powerful and precise instructions. "I'm now discovering new opportunities that would fetch in £3,750 per month" is a whole lot more exact than "I need more money."

Your RAS may still come up with a few totally useless suggestions. So you may find your eye caught by a book about how to train as an all-in wrestler, (when you're a 42-year old who weighs 7-and-a half stones) or how to have a lucrative career in accountancy (when you got a D on your Maths GCSE - and that was a long time ago) but it will improve with practice! Be open minded. You have set yourself a target of doing something different - so some of the opportunities that cross your path might be very different indeed. Don't automatically dismiss everything that seems a long way off what you have tried before. A course on "How to write a best-selling novel" might not be as ridiculous as you think. A flyer from the college about part-time classes to get a new qualification might have landed on your doormat for a reason. The friend who tells you about a network marketing opportunity might be worth listening to. Allow that inner guidance you said you were open to, to bring you into a much wider world.

Wendy Aridela

Using Both Sides of Your Brain

There are quite a few books out there on how to fix your money problems in a linear, left-brain kind of way. So they advise you how to set up a debt-repayment programme, how to budget, how to save and so on. (There's some of that in this book, in the section on Reprogramming the Physical Level) There's nothing wrong with these kinds of approaches - indeed, for some people, they may be exactly what is needed as the first step. However, I don't think they go far enough in themselves to be the whole answer.

For a start, if you have what Zig Ziglar used to refer to as "Stinkin' Thinking" you may find yourself back in a similar situation 6 months, 12 months, or a couple of years down the line. So you need to do the Mental Level reprogramming as well as working on the Physical Level. But also, these kinds of approaches are only using half your brain and I think it's important to use the other half, too!

As you may know, human brains look rather like a walnut, separated into two similar-looking halves, joined by a narrow bridge of nervous tissue. In general terms, the left-hand side of your brain deals with logic, plans, step-by-step processes, Mathematical thinking and things that can easily be put into words. Your right-brain, on the other hand, is more intuitive and holistic. It looks for patterns, sees the big picture, and finds solutions by sensing the way to something that *feels* right. It can be hard to put right-brain thinking into words because it's not really working on that kind of level. How do you know something is right for you? Often you *just do* - and can't say how you know. It feels right. You can't pin it down in words. That's right-brain thinking for you.

There are quite a lot of books out there that suggest right-brain approaches to working on your money-stuff - using Vision Boards, "magic", rituals and oracles for example. Again, there's nothing wrong with this kind of approach - except that, as before, you're only using half your brain! To reprogram your Money-Mind I think it seems like common sense to use both halves - after all, that's what they're there for. So let's look at how you can put together a more integrated approach for yourself.

Left Brain - Making Action Plans

I have to admit that I was 27 before I discovered the notion of planning my way to a different kind of life. Even more embarrassingly, my big AHA! moment didn't come from reading some wonderfully enlightened self-help book, but from Cosmopolitan magazine. They used to have a regular correspondent called Tom Crabtree, who wrote wise and witty little articles about coping with life. His

Wendy Aridela

article on Life-Planning changed my life, quite literally.

If your life is not what you want it to be, he wrote, stop moaning and complaining about it and start thinking what you'd like to have instead. Then start to do some sensible thinking about how to get from A to B. Break it down into little, bite-size steps and start moving. Take some action - this week - on the first step. Then, when you've done that, take step 2.

It may not be obvious right now what every single step you might have to take will be. There may be parts of the journey that still look a bit blurry on your plan. But as you take each step, you'll get clearer about the next step. You'll come across new information. It will become more obvious what are the questions you need to ask. You'll find out who to ask, or where to look. It will work out.

You may end up taking the odd detour that wasn't on your plan. That's OK. After all, think of driving from Plymouth to Glasgow. You may not know when you set off that part of the motorway is blocked by an accident. You may have to turn off the road to find petrol or to use the bathroom. It's all OK. If you just keep on driving, and following the map as well as you can, sooner or later, you'll reach Glasgow.

At the time I read the article, I had wanted for years to get a degree, but it didn't seem possible. I had three small children, the youngest of whom was still a baby and I lived 50 miles away from the nearest University. We couldn't move town because my husband was self-employed in a business that was just beginning to take off as he got known locally, so I'd felt trapped, obliged to put my plans on hold for maybe 5 or even 10 years.

That article hit me with about the same force you'd experience if the Angel Gabriel turned up at your door. I was galvanised! It honestly hadn't occurred to me to start investigating the possibilities because I'd just assumed it was impossible. I started researching. Which Universities could I get to fairly easily by train? (I didn't drive.) Could I claim a travel grant? Did Universities have crèches or day-nurseries? How much did they cost? What degrees could I study at accessible Universities? If I was leaving my house early each morning and getting back late each afternoon, how could I get the older kids to school? Who could help? Slowly, a plan came together, and just over a year later, I was attending University. It wasn't the easiest way to do it, perhaps, but I did it. If I could plan my way out of an "impossible" problem, can you?

To start with, you need to be clear about two things - where are you starting from? And where do you want to go? In other words, what is your A and what is your B? Then you need to map a route from A to B. It may seem at first as if the two points don't join up at all, but there's always a way if you look. You may need to ask some different questions or think about the whole issue differently, but, somehow, there will be a way. If it's not at all obvious what on Earth that could be, can you at least see the first few steps? You may not be able to see step 3 from here, but it might be clearly visible once you've taken steps 1 and 2.

And finding a creative pathway to join A and B is where your intuition comes in. Once your RAS knows what to look for (I want a route to B) you might be surprised what - and who - turns up. Information and helpful people appear out of the blue. Just at the last minute, when some step seems totally impossible - a solution comes along. You hit what seems to be a dead-end and have to change your plan - and discover an easier or more straightforward way to do things. Life can be most mysterious! Almost certainly, things won't go to plan. But having the plan will give you the courage and conviction to get started and a direction to travel in. After that, be prepared for the unexpected!

Left Brain - Planning SMART

If you're already familiar with SMART targets, you can skip this section - otherwise, you will find it really helpful. To create powerful plans, you need to make them SMART. This is not the same thing as smart (lower-case) meaning a clever plan. SMART (upper case) is an acronym which sets out what you need for a plan to be maximally effective. Let's look at what each letter stands for:

S	**S is for Specific**
	Are you crystal clear about what you're going for? As I said in another section, "I want more money," is *not* a specific target. Would finding 20p on the street be OK? Do you want a higher monthly income or are you after a one-off sum of money? How much, specifically, do you want to have? Would it be OK if it came to you as compensation for an accident or left to you when someone died? Are you willing to earn it? Would it be OK if you had to work 80 hours a week to get it? Be clear what you do want and what you don't want!
M	**M is for Measurable**
	Can you tell if your plan is working? How? If you have a plan that says "I want to lose 18 kilos," for example, you can weigh yourself each week. If you weigh less than last week, your plan is working. If you weigh more than last week it isn't - and that gives you useful feedback that you're headed in the wrong direction and need to tweak the plan. Be clear about how you'll know that you're headed in

the right direction. What can you measure or tick off on a list?

A | A is for Achievable

"I want to earn an extra £20,000 a year," may well be very achievable, especially if you make the time-scale for doing it realistic. "I want 2 million pounds by next Tuesday" is probably not! "I want to win an Olympic Gold medal" is probably not achievable if you're over 25. Do you see? Don't set yourself up to fail by setting unachievable goals. Boldness is one thing, but living in La-La land is something else!

R | R is for Relevant

It's no good creating an action plan that won't take you to where you want to go. So, for example, if you wanted to lose 18 kilos, some kind of eating plan is probably relevant. An exercise plan may be relevant. Building a new shelf unit and creating an intricate new filing system for your cook-books is *not* relevant. It may make you feel constructive and busy, but it won't get you started on losing that 18 kilos. Make sure that your plan will take you to your destination and is not just an elaborate smoke-screen for keeping your life the same!

Reprogramming your Money-Mind

T	**T is for Timed**
	You want to put some kind of time limit on your plan. Going back to our person who wants to lose 18 kilos, for example - if he or she lost 10 grams a month, they would indeed be on track for losing 18 kilos. However, it would take them over 100 years to do so! They'd almost certainly die before they achieved their goal. So you need some kind of realistic timescale on your plan and you need to schedule the steps to keep you more or less on track. As I've said, life may well intervene and push things off course a bit. You may not arrive at your B exactly on schedule - but the timescale element of your plan keeps you on track, with a clear goal.

Left Brain - Scheduling

You can have the clearest and most elegant plan in the Universe, but if you never get around to putting it into action, it's not going to get you to where you want to go. (Duh!) The best way to get yourself to take action is to schedule a clear time-slot for each step. Write it into your diary. Set a reminder on your phone. And then do it! If a real emergency crops up, you can set your plan on one side for however long it takes to sort out the crisis, but then get straight back to it. Don't let what Shakespeare called "the slings and arrows of outrageous fortune" derail you. Reschedule and keep taking action.

If you are like many people, with a busy life, it may be hard at first to carve out the time to put your plans into action. If this is true for you, use what I call "The Power of 1%" This is consciously using the knowledge that 15 minutes is 1% of your day. (after rounding up the decimals!) Make a decision that, from now on, 1% of every day is for you. Your family, friends and job can surely get by on 99% of you! (If they think they can't, you may need to insist!)

Use those 15 minutes every day to take another small step towards your goal. Yes, it's a tiny amount. But it adds up to over 90 hours a year - which is not a tiny amount. You can make a lot of changes in 90 hours! Schedule the action for each day in your diary or planner, so you don't waste time wondering what to do and then take those small steps, every day. The results can be astonishing!

Right Brain - Working with the Big Picture

OK, you've got your left-brain working for you. You've made your plan and you're working it. Now we stir some magic into the mix by adding in the right-brain! Using the right-brain is how you get over the gaps in the road where A doesn't seem to connect to B at all. It's also how you decide what to do when you hit a cross roads and you can't tell which of 2 or 3 roads to take to get to B.

The right-brain creates those astonishing synchronicities where it seems that you're in the right place at the right time for exactly the right thing to happen. So let's take a look at how you can turn up the volume and get it working for you to the max!

Because your right-brain works in a more holistic way than the left-brain, it's good at sensing the Big Picture. Your left-brain is like someone following a map. It will tell you "Go down Grosvenor Street and turn right onto Chantry Road." The right-brain is like one of those people with an in-built sense of direction They look around and point, saying "We need to be over there."

Which means that the right-brain is just what you need if you reach a dead-end or the path you're on seems to peter out. If it's not obvious what to do, take note of what your options are. It may - at this point - seem that *none of them* is going to take you where you want to go, but don't worry.

Suppose you have 3 options, which (being totally original) I'll call 1, 2 and 3. Imagine choice 1 as a little picture. This might be a picture of an action to take, or a picture of a path or some symbol that represents your choice. Mentally put your choice 1 picture on one of your outstretched hands. Now imagine choice 2 as a little picture. Again, it may be a picture of an action or a symbolic picture such as one of a path. Mentally hold that picture on your other hand. Now bring both hands up together in front of your eyes so you can see both pictures at once. (Yes, I know these are imaginary pictures, but, on some level, you can clearly see both of them!)

Now, without much thought, ask yourself which picture looks or feels lighter. You may mentally *see* this as lighter - in the sense of one picture having more sunshine in it than the other. Or you may *feel* it as lighter, in the sense of one picture seeming to weigh less than the other. Whichever way it happens, the lighter picture is the better choice, so let the heavier/darker one go. Now make a picture of choice 3 and hold it next to the picture which was the lightest one so far. Is choice 3 lighter or darker than your first picture. Heavier or lighter? Again, keep the lighter picture and let the heavier/darker one go.

Your right-brain has compared your options against its sense that you need to get to "over there" and has computed your best path. However weird it seems, go with that choice. You may well find some completely unexpected option opening out a little way down the path, or find that this path leads you to someone who can help in a practical way. Trust, and keep walking forwards, keeping your awareness

Reprogramming your Money-Mind

of your destination in the back of your mind. The more you use your right-brain awareness in this way, the clearer your guidance will become.

Wendy Aridela

Right Brain - Sleep on It!

While you sleep, your whole brain works on making sense of your day. It joins the dots that connect your experience with your beliefs. It fills in some of the missing bits of stories. It comes up with explanations. And it solves problems. Your right brain is especially skilled at solving your problems in the form of dreams. It turns your challenges into stories and then acts out different scenarios in your mind to find the best solutions.

I'm sure you've had the experience of going to bed with some kind of problem and waking up in the morning with an answer, even if that's only happened once or twice in your life. But you can harness this ability to quite consciously and deliberately seek guidance. Exactly how you go about this depends on you. Some people find it's enough simply to ask the question inside their own mind before they settle down to sleep. Other people find it works better to write out their question on a piece of paper and put it under their pillow. Some people go even further and add something symbolic - maybe an amethyst crystal or an angel card - to make it very clear to themselves that this is a formal request for help, information or guidance. Try doing it in several different ways, perhaps, to find what works best for you.

Reprogramming your Money-Mind

One point it's worth making is that your right-brain doesn't have the same sense of time as your left-brain. Clocks and calendars are left-brain inventions - the right-brain doesn't run on Tidy-Time like that! So don't be surprised if you don't always get an answer the first night of asking. It may take several night before your right-brain slowly sifts through the possibilities. Or you may have to wait for a New Moon or a Full Moon for your right-brain to do its magic and give you the answer you want. Don't doubt! Sooner or later, the answer will come!

Section 2
Reprogramming the Spiritual Level

SECTION TWO - Reprogramming the spiritual level

What this section is about

For some people, the spiritual level contains their greatest blocks to a more prosperous and abundant life. Many religious traditions clearly separate the spiritual world from the material. They believe that God and money can't really even be spoken of in the same breath. You certainly can't be a "true believer" and be in serious pursuit of wealth. For them, there's a choice - you value God *or* you value money. You can't have both.

At the same time, it's often these same religions that are endlessly asking their supporters for alms, donations or tithes. It's all somewhat confusing, to say the least! How can you support your church if you've embraced poverty? How can you respond to disasters, help the homeless, feed the starving or change the world if you don't have any money? If you go without, does that make the world more fair for everyone else?

Obviously, it's not my intent to undermine your religious beliefs in any way. What you believe is your business, not mine. But in this section, I put forward some ideas you might like to consider. You don't have to believe they are true. But you might find that they are useful!

Wendy Aridela

You Are God's Adventure

Health Warning!

Some of the ideas is this section are likely to be new to you so I'm letting you know that *I* know that they may sound a bit weird. Quite often, our reaction to startlingly new beliefs is just to reject them out of hand. Relax! I'm not asking you to change your beliefs, here. You don't have to believe that any of the ideas in this section are *true* - although I totally believe them. Instead, read this section and ask yourself whether or not any of these ideas could be *useful* for you. Don't make a decision yet as to whether these ideas are true or false. Put them in your mental filing tray marked *"for consideration"* or *"pending"* and leave them there for a few weeks.

Take the time to play about with them. Every now and again, let them roll over your mind in the same way you might roll a fine wine around your mouth to pick up the layers of flavour. Give the occasional 5 or 10 minutes to thinking through how your life would feel different if this section *were* true. How might you look at your life differently? Which bits of your life would you see *most* differently? How would that change how you feel about those incidents, those people, those events? And how does that change how you feel about yourself? After you've played about with these ideas for a while you can decide that, yes, they seem helpful and so decide to

Reprogramming your Money-Mind

incorporate them into your inner map of the world. Or you can decide that, no, they don't feel helpful, and go back to how you saw things before - for now. (You may want to rethink them a few months down the line, or even a few years - and that's OK, too.) I just want to be sure that you give yourself this chance to see the whole of your life in a radically new way. These ideas may not at first seem to be anything about money, but bear with me - they are. This section connects to *everything* in your life.

Why the heck are you here?

Probably most of us have asked ourselves this question or something along the same lines, at least once or twice in our lives. Why are we here? What on Earth is life all about? Why is all this *stuff* happening to me? The world's religions and philosophies have come up with a variety of answers, some of which are perhaps more helpful than others.

- Life's a vale of tears (Not very helpful!)
- Life is a test. if you pass, you get to go to Heaven when you die. If you fail, you go to Hell.
- Life is a learning process (Great - but what am I meant to be learning?)
- Life is a punishment for the bad stuff you did in previous lifetimes (So what did I do so wrong, last time round?)

- Life is suffering (Well, that makes me feel a whole lot better - NOT!)
- Life is a process of perfecting yourself. After repeated lifetimes, you get perfect enough to not have to do it any more.
- Life is pointless. We're here as an evolutionary accident when a cosmic ray or something mutated a bunch of monkeys and made them clever enough to turn into humans.

You get the idea. And you probably have some thoughts of your own about all this. I'd like to suggest an alternative. You're a spiritual being, here on an adventure! Let me tell you where I got such an idea from in the first place and let's consider it in a bit more depth.

How I came up with such a mad idea

The idea of being here on an adventure came to me in stages, as a result of several powerful meditation experiences, spread over a number of years. And I assure you, I didn't find it easy to accept, especially to begin with. The first meditation experience came at a difficult time in my life when I was going through a lot of changes. I'd got divorced, I'd started work at a job that was turning out to be less enjoyable than I'd expected and moved towns (to start the new job.) This meant I was living in a big city where I had almost no friends. On top of all that,

I found myself the single parent of three teenage children who were all having their own difficulties in coping with the divorce and the move away from all of their friends. Life was challenging, to put it mildly!

I started asking myself "Why am I here?" in a big way. It really was a burning question. My life felt as if it had gone off track and I was no longer sure what I was meant to be doing. You may have gone through times like this, yourself - times when it doesn't simply seem that the goal-posts seem to have moved, but you thought you were playing football and suddenly you seem to be on a cricket pitch?

Anyway, that's the kind of space I was in when I sat down to meditate and had a totally out-of-the-blue experience. Normally, when I meditated, I'd have a sense of inner light. I'd sit in it and allow it to fill me up. The whole thing would last maybe 30 or 45 minutes and I'd get up feeling more peaceful, centred and refreshed.

However, on this particular day, I found myself reliving a powerful memory of the time before I was born. I had just finished planning this lifetime. To make it clear to you how very odd this was, I had no concept at that time that I *had* planned this life. I had no clue that it was anything to do with me. I still assumed that life was pretty much something that just happened to you, willy-nilly. If I'd thought about it at all, I might have come up with the notion that maybe *God* had planned it all, somehow - it's reassuring to think that it all makes sense to *someone* - but certainly, it could be nothing to do with me! After all, if I'd planned my own life, surely I'd have arranged to have a better time of it? Wouldn't I have planned a lifetime of ease and comfort? Surely, I'd have given myself kinder parents, a happier marriage, more money and a more attractive body? So none of this could be my fault - only an idiot would wish a life this hard on themselves! I want you to understand how much this meditation experience was not only a complete surprise, but a quite unwelcome one.

Some people have suggested to me that I may have imagined the whole thing. All I can say is that it felt more real than remembering my first day at school. It felt more real than remembering my wedding or the births of my children. It had that solid kind of clunk to it that left absolutely no doubt in my mind that this had happened. Also, it's hard to understand why or how I'd imagine something I had no concept of at all. As I said, I not only didn't have a clue that I'd planned this lifetime but I had no notion that lifetimes might be planned at all - by anyone.

But in my meditation, there I was, having just planned this lifetime. I was in some vast, light-filled space. I had a sense of myself as a clearly defined person, yet that wasn't exactly the Wendy Aridela I am now. I didn't seem to have a physical body - I seemed to be made of light. But if I'd had a physical face, I'd have been grinning all over it. I was absolutely delighted with what I'd just set up for myself. Honestly, overjoyed is not too strong a word for it - I was ecstatic! If I'd been using human speech, I'd have been leaping about, shouting "Woo-hoo!" (Instead, there was a kind of wordless equivalent - a feeling that simply poured out of me.)

Can you imagine how excited you'd be if you were a highly skilled mountaineer and you'd just had the phone call to tell you a big company had agreed to sponsor your expedition to Everest? The dream of a lifetime, the ultimate thrill? The challenge that would be the crowning point of your climbing career? Or, if you can't imagine the thrill of extreme sports, suppose you played in a band and someone had just sponsored a nationwide tour. It was something like that.

When I came out of the meditation, I was devastated! What! I'd planned this? Heavens above, what had I been thinking of? Is it possible for spiritual beings to be mad as a box of frogs? Because I must have been! The experience had been so real, so *normal*, somehow, that I didn't doubt it for a moment. But it made no sense at all. It undermined the foundations of my world. What on Earth had inspired me to choose such a complicated and difficult life? Why would *anyone* choose challenges over ease, a trek through Nepal rather than a beach holiday in the Maldives?

So, for a moment, put yourself in my shoes at this point. Why would you - the Real You, the Big You - have chosen *your* life? Assuming there must be a good reason behind it, and that your Real Self is not either nuts or nasty, what have you gained so far from living the life you've led rather than some other life? You may well not know - I certainly didn't. It took me another couple of decades and several more out-of-the-blue meditation experiences to fill in the missing bits of the jigsaw.

In one sense, of course, this experience was very empowering because it pushed me to make sense of my life. If your life has been planned by someone else - God, your Guardian Angel, or even the Tooth Fairy (honestly, it can seem like that, sometimes!) then it's understandable that it makes no kind of sense to you. After all, who knows what God had in mind? Or maybe your Guardian Angel has an odd sense of humour?

But if your life has been planned by *you*, then on some very deep level, it all makes sense to you. Underneath all your thoughts and ideas about it, you do really know why you're here. Not consciously, maybe - but the understanding must be in there, somewhere.

Reprogramming your Money-Mind

I found it *helpful* to believe this - remember what I said about some beliefs being helpful even when you can't be absolutely certain whether or not they are true? I still wasn't certain of my motivation, though. I'd seemed very happy and joyous in my meditation but maybe because that was because I'd arranged to pile my plate so full that I'd pay off all the karmic debts from 30 lifetimes of bad behaviour? Maybe I was balancing the cosmic books in some way? It had felt as if I'd planned a lifetime of incredible joy for myself - but there was obviously a missing jigsaw piece or two, because it wasn't very like that right now.

One of the key pieces came about eight years later. I was meditating as usual when I suddenly found myself in a much deeper place and I *knew* - with my whole being - that I was totally and completely loved. In this wonderful space, I could see that, not only was God "on my side" but that every single bit of my life was a gift to me. Everything. Every single thing was an outpouring of love to me. Even the most difficult things - they were opportunities to bring old pain to the surface for healing or offered a chance to go beyond my previous ideas about myself and release strengths and talents I never knew I had. Every single thing was for my benefit.

I came out of that meditation and cried for about half-an-hour. I hadn't realised up until then how much I had still been believing, at the back of my mind, in the God of my childhood who sat in the sky, just waiting to punish me for being such a bad person. I hadn't realised what a weight I'd been carrying, until I let it go. If you'd asked me before that whether or not I believed in a kind and loving God, I'd almost definitely have said "yes." After all, we all know that's the right answer. But knowing it's the right answer and *knowing* it - in your bones - turn out to be two very different things.

And knowing in your bones that God is for you, not against you, changes all of life. Because all of us have challenges. Even those of us who do seem to have chosen lives that are a beach holiday on the Maldives must have days when the wind blows sand onto your ice-cream or a seagull poos on your hair! Everyone has bad days. Everyone has hard times. And at such times, it's tempting to look around at other people and to say to yourself, "Well, how come *they* don't seem to have hard times like this? How come *they* don't have my problems? How come *they* get to be happier than *me*?" It's tempting to want your problems to go away and to have their beach-holiday life, isn't it? Which brings us back to the adventure.

Why pick a life of challenges?

When you were a kid, did you ever have a teacher who gave you work that was too easy? Maybe you had a supply teacher come in one day when your usual teacher was off sick, who kept you busy all day with colouring and "baby-work?" For a day, having work like that can be fun - a break from the pressure. But if your teacher was away for a few days, how did you feel after several days of colouring and 2+2 Maths? Bored sick, I would guess, or at least pretty fed up.

Similarly, how did you feel if, year after year, you didn't get picked for a speaking part in the class Christmas play, but (once again) got to be one of the Christmas trees in the background? You knew you'd make a great inn-keeper, or felt confident you could play Archangel Gabriel, but there you were again, with that silly pointy green hat on your head, and draped in tinsel, with nothing else to do but join in the chorus of "We wish you a merry Christmas?" Humans have an inbuilt drive to grow and learn - to be more and do more - and we get bored and demotivated when we can't follow it.

There's a satisfaction to doing a job for yourself, getting it done, and looking around with pride at your finished handiwork, isn't there? Whether you've just baked a cake, knitted a sweater for your best-beloved, built a bookcase or painted the living-room, there's a satisfaction that you don't get from serving up a store-bought cake, buying a new jumper for your partner, getting a bookcase from the furniture shop, or having the decorators in to do your living-room for you. The ready-made options may still feel good and you may enjoy them, but there's a real added joy in being able to say "I did it myself."

It's like that with life. We choose challenges because we're ready for them. On some level we not only enjoy them, we *thrive* on them. We don't want a life that's just like lying on a beach. We're fed up with colouring and 2+2. We've been lifting the light weights in the gym to the point where we can do 50 reps without breaking a sweat. We want more. Every single one of us chooses our challenges because we're ready for them. We're brave. We're up for it. We're here on a spiritual adventure. We want the excitement. We may not be 100% sure that we can do it, but we're ready to try! Try what? you might ask. What I eventually came to see was that I'm here to learn to be me - and all of life is conspiring with me to help me do it as well as humanly possible. You're here to learn to be you.

What you really want, on a soul-level, is to be the brightest, shiniest, biggest version of you that you could possibly be. Why? Because this lets more of your Real Self flow out into the world. It allows the Divine energy in you to act on and in the world - through you. When you are being the brightest version of you that you can be, it's like being a cable plugged into the mains. Enormous voltages of Divine energy get to pour through you - and that feels absolutely fantastic!

Reprogramming your Money-Mind

That energy may come through you as creativity. It could manifest as healing abilities. You might paint, or compose music, or write poetry. Or when you're totally "plugged in" you become a wise problem-solver or therapist, with an almost intuitive feel for what to say next. Maybe in you it comes through as care and compassion or as an amazing feel for combining simple, nutritious ingredients into wonderfully tasty meals. Maybe you have a "feel" for wood or a "knack" with engines?

But you know when you're really connected to your Real Self because those are the occasions when you lose all sense of time and do your very best work. You're on track. You're in the zone. And sometimes, the work you do in those states delights and astonishes even you. What you do when you're plugged in and switched on is to become a channel for your own indwelling brilliance to emerge into the world.

Wendy Aridela

Becoming who you are

Acorns will try their hardest to grow into oak trees, come what may. If they fall into a crack in a cliff face by the edge of the sea, it may take them years to grow even ten feet tall. They may be twisted out of shape by the winds, wizened and dwarfed by the harsh conditions, but they are committed to their destiny. They have an inner drive to express the oak-tree-ness that is their Inner Self. It's the same with us. We have an inner drive to become all of who we really are. And just as there are some tree seeds that need a forest-fire to make them germinate, we often need challenges to shake us out of limiting patterns of behaviour and belief and to open us up to more of our own magnificence.

And that's where we're all headed - magnificence. Your Real Self is amazing. You have a Light and a Love within you deeper and brighter than anything you have ever imagined. You are stronger than you believe. You have gifts you haven't even begun to suspect. Your real abundance in life is *you*. And it's because you know this on a deep level that you are prepared to go through some pretty dramatic stuff to let that amazingness and abundance out.

So how do you do that? How do you release that abundance within? Look at what you love to do, and start from there. You don't enjoy every activity equally - some things are more *you*. They resonate with you. You know you do them well. I love sewing, for example. I like to make patchwork quilts. I love making dolls and toys for my grandchildren. I enjoy making clothes and soft furnishings. I also like to write and get great pleasure from it. I love stringing words together and enjoy reading through what I've written and appreciating that I've explained something clearly. I enjoy public speaking, especially when I can make people laugh. I love writing courses and programmes and teaching them. But I'm not a brilliant cook at all and I don't particularly enjoy cooking. Similarly, I have zero affinity with car engines and can't bear to have oil on my hands so mechanical activities are really not my thing.

My guess is that you are the same - you have real gifts and talents for some activities while there are other things you don't enjoy or just can't seem to get the knack of. What if this isn't an accident? What if all of life has been a training program designed to develop in you a unique set of skills, talents and knowledge that nobody else can combine in quite the same way?

There are a lot of other writers on the planet. There are even lots who write about money. There may be several hundred who write about money from a spiritual perspective. But I'm the only one who writes like me, explaining things from my point of view. Some people may get some useful ideas from my books, but get more from reading books written by other authors. But there will be a few people for whom what I write completely touches them. In that moment, I am the solution to their problems. I am the answer they have been looking for. It is the same in your life. Somewhere, somehow, your skills and talents combine to make you somebody's perfect solution. This doesn't mean you now have to save the world or feed the starving. You don't have to become the Prime Minister or Mother Teresa. Your challenge is simply to be you - but to be the you that you really are deep down inside. Because as you do that, you help other people to connect more deeply with who they really are.

Your Reflection in the World

Which brings us to money. Because the outside world will always reflect who you are. Imagine you are looking in a mirror. How do you make the reflection smile at you? Would you stand tickling the mirror? Would you tell your reflection some jokes? Could you make your reflection smile by trying to pull its mouth into a smiling shape? Obviously not! We all know that the way to make your reflection smile is to smile. The reflection will mirror whatever your face is doing. You can't change the reflection without changing yourself - and then the reflection changes instantly.

It's the same with life. Common sense tells us that the way to change the circumstances of our life is to

Reprogramming your Money-Mind

take action. Do something! Change something! And obviously, up to a point, it's true. But have you ever read about the people who win the Lottery and have lost it all within a year or two? Or rock stars who make it big and then somehow sabotage themselves with drink, drugs, or crazy living so that they end up prematurely dead or else living in a trailer park, looking about thirty years older than they actually are?

You can't end up living a life that's bigger than you think *you* are. You'll always act to "cut yourself back down to size." The first step in living a bigger life - and that certainly includes a life with more money - is to allow yourself to be a bigger person. Step up. Let your light shine out. Discover more of the amazing abundance that you are. Work on discovering your gifts. Share who you are with the world. Help more people. Make a bigger difference. Allow the challenges in your life to open you up and grow you. Don't hold back. Put your heart into what you do. Smile more. Have more fun. Bring more joy.

And what happens as you do is that the outside world starts to mirror the abundance within. When you breathe out , you make space for fresh oxygenated air to flow in. If you don't breathe out the stale air you have inside you, no more oxygenated air can get in - there's no space. To illustrate this, you might like to try this breathing meditation.

81

Wendy Aridela

Focusing on Breathing

Sit quietly and simply pay attention to your breathing. You don't need to do anything to it. Just notice how you breathe. Breathing is a wonderful mirror of our energy interactions with the world. So just sit, and pay attention to your breathing - don't try to change it, just have the intention to notice what you're doing.

Do you tend to hold your breath? Or breath out too much so that every now and again, you find yourself needing to take in a big breath like a gasp, to catch up? Do you keep yourself waiting, with empty lungs, before you let yourself breath in again? Do you breathe shallowly - little breaths in and out, instead of letting yourself take the big deep breaths that would relax and nourish you?

Whatever you notice, don't beat yourself up, or try to 'fix' it - just keep breathing. And notice how- if you will allow it, over time, your breathing will tend to come into balance almost by itself. And afterwards, reflect. It's often interesting when you see a connection between how you breathe and how you give and receive in the world.

It's the same with abundance. As you share your gifts with the world, you're letting your Light and Love and all-round fantastic shininess out into the world. And the world will respond by sending *its* light and love and shininess back into your life. Some of this may come as praise, some may come as smiles, some may come as appreciation - but some will definitely come as money.

Just as when you breathe, you tend to get the same amount back in that you allow out. The brighter you shine, the more you spread joy, the more people you help, the more problems you solve, the bigger the difference that you make - the more abundance flows back to you. Which nicely leads us on to the next problem that could be holding you back from a life of greater abundance and prosperity.

How good are you at receiving?

"Ask and you shall receive." That's what the Bible tells us. But some people are asking and asking - even shouting at the Universe - while standing with their hands firmly held behind their back. You can't receive unless you have an openness to do so. So this is a good time to take an honest look at yourself and to ask how good you are at receiving.

Let's start with compliments. Someone tells you they like the way you've done your hair. Or they tell you that the colour you're wearing makes you look great. How do you respond? Honestly? If you're like a lot of people you probably deflect the compliment with a comment such as "This old thing? I've had it for years." Or you may be able to accept it and say "Thank you," but then feel so uncomfortable you have to quickly change the subject. Is this ringing any bells?

What happens if you give someone a lift and they offer you some petrol money? Can you accept that? What about someone who brings you a bunch of flowers or a box of chocolates after you've done a good turn? How does that feel? What happens if someone asks you to help them mend their car/ fix their computer/ shorten a pair of curtains - and asks you how much you want to be paid for it? How easy is it to set a price? Do you feel as if you're exploiting them or ripping them off if you ask for a fair market price for your labour? Can you see that your openness to receive may - ever so occasionally - be somewhat less than 100%?

Being open to opportunities

I remember someone who came on one of my Abundance programmes. She was a Primary school teacher on a fixed salary and couldn't see how she could get more money flowing in. In the course of discussion one day, she mentioned that every day she made up a story to tell to the children in her class in the half-hour before home-time. The children loved these stories and had been so enthusiastic about them to their parents that several mums had asked whether she made CDs of the stories, as they'd be happy to buy them.

"Wow!" I said. "So are you going to record some CDs?"

"No," she replied. "I mean, you can't sell to *parents*, can you?"

I pointed out that, while school etiquette may suggest that transacting personal business on the school premises wasn't acceptable, she had several other options. One might be to split all the proceeds 50:50 with the school. If half the cash went into school funds, I thought she might find that the Headteacher suddenly became more enthusiastic! Otherwise, there was nothing to stop her selling CDs on Ebay or Amazon and simply giving parents the link.

But as she was on an Abundance programme and had said she wanted more cash, I didn't think it was a coincidence that this idea had come up. Nonetheless, she decided that she didn't want to follow up because it wasn't what she'd had in mind when she said she wanted more money coming in!

Has anything like this ever happened to you? You express a desire for more money and then, often within a few days, some new opportunity crops up? However, although it lies well within your capabilities, it's not what you usually do. It's not your normal way of receiving money, so you say No. This is what I mean when I say that before more abundance can flow into your life, you have to expand your view of yourself to allow more abundance to flow out.

Abundance is a 2-way street. It's not just about the cash that flows into your life - it's about the skills, talents and expertise you flow out, too. Have the confidence to allow yourself to shine! At first, all the opportunities you get may just be small ones. But some of the world's big businesses started off in just this way - someone making their own cosmetics at the kitchen table, baking cakes for neighbours, designing a business leaflet for a friend. By learning to be open to receive, who knows what you are opening the door to?

Money as a Spiritual Practice

This is an idea you may like to play with. At first it may seem somewhat shocking -we are so used to the notion of dividing the world into spiritual stuff and non-spiritual stuff, and money definitely comes into the non-spiritual box, doesn't it? But actually, life is a seamless whole. Everything is Divine energy, in one form or another. And that definitely includes money.

On one level, all of life is about expanding our capacity to allow Divine energy to flow through us, to heal and bless the world in all we do. We can see that easily when we do meditations to open up to light or love. It feels wonderful! We're designed to open to more light and more light. So why do we suddenly dig in our heels when that Divine energy is in the form of money?

"Whoah!" we say, "Money is different. Money is real. Money needs to be under control. I can't just open up to the flow of money. That would make me materialistic. I can't do that! It's against my spiritual values." My question is simple. How is money different? What would happen in your life if you allowed yourself to open to the flow of money - *as Divine energy*?

You don't feel obliged to push away the flow of breath into your body in case it makes you into the wrong kind of person. Neither do you feel compelled to hold onto it, in case no more flows your way for a while. What if you could treat money in the same way? What if you could learn to spot your fear and guilt and shame around money and work with it, until you could allow money to flow freely through your life, in the same way you allow air to do?

What if you were to use money as an indicator of how well you had learned to trust the Universe? And as a marker of how clearly you were aligning with guidance? What if you experimented with believing that all your needs really were met? And that the Universe would offer you a constant stream of opportunities to flow your gifts and skills out to the world and have money flow in, in exchange, if you learnt to follow the subtle nudges of your inner guidance system?

Obviously, it's up to you whether - and how- you follow up these suggestions. But, in my own life, starting to work with money as a spiritual practice has made an enormous difference. For years, I had my life so tidily organised into boxes, with money in its own box, well away from spiritual things. And then I began to feel that I wanted my spiritual practice to encompass all of my life. I didn't want any areas of my life to be on the outside.

Deciding to work on reprogramming my Money-Mind felt like a big step. Money was such a taboo area. But I've released more fear, shame and guilt since I've been working with money than in the whole of my spiritual practice beforehand. I've opened to levels of trust in the Universe I couldn't have imagined before. And I feel that my life now is so rich. I have finally been able to allow myself to feel really loved. I have allowed myself to feel cared for and nurtured. And, for me, that has been massive. If you're reading this, maybe there's something here for you? Maybe life is offering you an opportunity?

The Law of Attraction - the Simple Version

The idea of being open to opportunities leads in well to some discussion about the Law of Attraction. If you read self-help books or surf the web, you are likely to have come across this. It's often expressed in quotes such as:
"Thoughts become things." or
"You become what you think about, all day long."

The Law of Attraction, as it's commonly explained, suggests that everything in the Universe, even when it appears to be solid matter, is actually made from vibrating energy. This is not some weird woo-woo idea, incidentally, but is accepted as true in the studies of atomic Physics. Because everything is vibrating, everything is said to have a characteristic frequency. There's a certain common-sense validity to this. It makes sense that a butterfly is vibrating at a different frequency from a tractor, for example - they are just totally different things!

In the same way, thoughts - which can be physically represented by an EEG (electroencephalograph) machine as brainwaves of varying frequencies - also have characteristic frequencies. The brainwaves of a meditator, experiencing deep relaxation and calm, are different from those of a person who is feeling stressed and anxious. In fact the difference is so great that it can be easily identified even by high school students learning about brainwaves for the first time!

The insight behind the Law of Attraction is that these two sets of frequencies are connected. Thoughts are creative. What you think affects what comes into your life. We've already seen - in the Mental Level section - how your Reticular Activating System (RAS) alerts you to notice more of the people, things and events that seem to hold an emotional charge for you, whether that is positive or negative. This tends to create self-fulfilling prophecies in your life. So if you have the belief that blonde women are silly and stupid, you'll tend to notice blonde women doing and saying foolish things - while missing both the intelligent blonde women around you and the silly brunettes.

If you believe that the state of the economy means that you'd be crazy to start a new business now because it would definitely fail, you'll notice all the news items about foreclosures, bankruptcies, and redundancies, while failing to spot the businesses that are thriving despite - or even because of - the downturn.

The premise of the Law of Attraction is that, by changing what you focus your thoughts upon, you can change what turns up in your life. Up to a point, this is uncontroversial. For example, let's suppose that the "blondist" person in our example meets a very attractive blonde woman and starts dating. Much to his or her surprise, they come to see that this woman is not only good-looking, but is also witty and intelligent! At first, they may choose to see their date as an exception to the rule, but what is likely to happen then is that they come across more and more 'exceptions'. Once they have a mental category of 'blonde women who are exceptions to the "dizzy-blonde" rule', they'll find more of them. Eventually, the day may come when our "blondist" person comes to see that the world is full of intelligent blonde women! They come to see that intelligence is not correlated with hair colour at all. And their experience now reflects their new beliefs. They meet intelligent people and unintelligent people with every possible hair colour. So far, so good.

But what about the books and websites that seem to suggest that if you want a new car, all you have to do is to focus your thoughts upon it and it will turn up in your life? Some internet "experts" seem to be saying that the Law of Attraction can be used to turn your whole life into a giant vending machine. You simply pop in the right thought and out pops a new car - or a house, a Soulmate, a Lottery win, or anything else that may cross your mind. Their idea is that thoughts will tend to 'magnetise' people, events, things and opportunities on the same frequency. So if you hold onto a thought about a new car, it will attract a new car to you. Well, if you've tried it, you know that it's not as simple as that!

Yes, thought is creative. But *every* thought is creative - and psychologists have estimated that we think about 60,000 thoughts a day. So if you spend 10 minutes every day focusing on a new car, but then spend the next 15 *hours* worrying about your lack of money, how badly your life is going, how you never seem to get what you want, and how much you *need* a new car (desperately!) because your old one is leaking oil and is likely to go wrong soon in any one of a dozen different ways, each of which you worry about in detail, how likely do you think it is that a new car will turn up? You have drowned out your new car thoughts in a tide of worry! But also, it turns out that you may have misunderstood what the Law of Attraction could really be about, and how it can be a very useful tool in your spiritual growth and development.

The Law of Attraction for Grown-Ups

The Law of Attraction is based on spiritual insight that everything is One. On a fundamental level, the energy that everything is made of is the *same* energy. It's all one thing. It's all joined up. This means that on the deepest level, you're not just *connected* to everything else, in the way that a balloon might be tied to a fence. You're an *integral part* of everything. We're all manifestations of the same underlying field of energy.

Because of this, everything works together. Everything works according to the same rules. If you drop an apple, it falls to the ground, because it is affected by gravity. But you could also drop a brick, a dog, or your granny and they'd *all* be affected by gravity. It isn't the case that some things are affected by gravity and some things aren't. In a similar way, *all* molecules move faster when they are hot than when they are cold.

When you look, the same patterns recur throughout Nature at lots of different levels. The patterns made as tree branches fan out from the trunk are similar to the branching patterns found in the leaf-veins - and are also similar to the branching patterns in river deltas, and the patterns in your blood vessels.

So, the deeper level of understanding the Law of Attraction is a recognition that on a deep level, your world is a reflection of who you are. Not just your thoughts, not just your feelings, but your world reflects your whole self. The outside reflects the inside, to a degree we usually don't notice. This gives each of us an amazing spiritual opportunity. The whole world around us becomes a way of increasing awareness of ourselves and expressing more of our deepest potential. The whole world, our whole life, becomes a spiritual gift.

Wendy Aridela

So, how can "Grown-Ups" use the Law of Attraction?

I don't want you to get the impression from this that I believe that the Law of Attraction doesn't work. It does work - but you need to understand that it works at more than one level.

Victim Level - at this level, people have no belief at all in the Law of Attraction. They believe that life is something that "just happens" to them. Events turn up in their lives, willy-nilly, whether they were wanted or unwanted. Thoughts can't possibly affect the real world, and all this woo-woo stuff is utter rubbish they declare - and so they continue to experience all the ups and downs of life at random. Their only control over life is to work harder, plan in more detail and possibly, to worry more!

Technician Level - these people *get* the Law of Attraction enough to make it work for them, at least some of the time. They've understood that thinking worrying thoughts such as "I bet there's a traffic jam, I hope there isn't a traffic jam, There's almost always a traffic jam at this time of day - I hope I can avoid the traffic jam......" is as likely to result in them being stuck in a traffic jam as wishing "Wow! I'd love a traffic jam to happen!"

They recognise that focusing on what they *don't* want has similar outcomes to focusing on what they *do* want - more of that thing comes into their life, because that's what they are paying attention to. So they are learning to choose their thoughts carefully. They are learning to notice and let go of thoughts about what they don't want and to consciously choose thoughts and feelings about what they do want.

It can feel at times as if they are pushing against the flow. Determinedly reciting affirmations, creating vision boards and visualising their desired outcomes, they can sometimes be so determined to take their life in the direction they have planned that they fail to notice all kinds of ways in which life is trying to steer them in a different direction - one which could have a better outcome or which could lead to deeper growth and learning.

They may get what they want only to discover, sometimes, that it doesn't bring the happiness and fulfilment they were expecting it to bring. Or they may find that they can manifest some kinds of things but not others. So they always get a parking space, for example, but can't seem to get a regular flow of paying customers. Or they're good at manifesting money, but can't seem to get rewarding relationships sorted out. But, on the whole, technicians are competent manifestors.

Magician Level - once people can use the Law of Attraction effectively, they have entered on a path of self-discovery. What happens next is that they'll start to notice times when it doesn't seem to be working for them, no matter what they do. These times are invitations from the Universe to explore their beliefs, investigate their values, dive into their family stories or to simply learn new skills. As they do so, they break through blocks and find that they are suddenly succeeding on a deeper level or to a much greater degree than they would previously have believed possible.

They begin to see that all the apparent road-blocks are actually opportunities to step up and get *more* of what they want - not less. It becomes more and more apparent that the Universe is really on their side. They begin to develop new levels of trust as they see that what appear to be dead-ends may simply be diversions onto a slightly different route- one that wasn't in their "Master-Plan" but which seems to lead them to a more fulfilling outcome.

They start to get interested in where the Universe might be taking them - where this new path might lead. They begin to get insights that their Higher Self's vision for their life isn't just about them *having* more and *doing* more but is all about *being* more. Because, ultimately, that's what the Law of Attraction turns out to be about.

Magicians come to see that life doesn't reflect what they think so much as it reflects who they are. So the way to have more and to do more is to become a bigger version of yourself - the version of yourself for whom doing and having the life you imagine comes naturally.

Life becomes a path to expressing the very best of who you are - and as such, it brings you the greatest possible joy. It's also in the nature of things that a life expressing the very best of who you are tends to bring you more abundance of all kinds - from job satisfaction, to fame and fortune, to spiritual growth.

There are many people who believe that being on a spiritual path involves making a choice between a growing bank balance and a deepening level of insight, enlightenment and understanding. But actually, there is no need for this choice. Opening to a life of deep trust in Spirit and an ever-greater commitment to joy and gratitude can go hand in hand with a life that is also nurturing on every level - one in which we increasingly come to see that all our needs *are* truly met.

Magicians recognise that - far from choosing a materialistic life over a more spiritual one - they are using their exploration of money and success as part of their spiritual path. They are using it to deepen their connection with Divine creative energy, not to turn their back on it.

They recognise that money is just another form of Divine energy, another version of solidified light. And they understand that if their intention is to open up to Light, to become channels for a greater flow of Light through themselves and out into the world, they can't be totally closed to Light in the form of money. They see that money can be a part of the pattern of their life - a sustaining and nurturing blessing in the same way that food is, or breathing or companionship. And just as it's possible to change an unhealthy relationship with food into one that supports and nourishes the unique patterns of our own DNA, so it's possible to change an unhealthy relationship with money into one that maximises our spiritual potential rather than limits it.

Magicians recognise that, held within the Creative Field, there is a perfect pattern for their life. This is the pattern that they themselves created with input from angels, guides and teachers, before they came into incarnation. It holds the energy template for all the possibilities they can bring into being in this lifetime. Like a priceless diamond that can be cut in different ways, to bring out different facets of its brilliance, the Perfect Pattern can be applied to life more or less skilfully, with more or less brilliance - but it will still always be - recognisably - the same pattern.

Whether or not you can accept this is true, it can be the most amazingly helpful and useful belief to hold. Because this Perfect Pattern isn't just some generic "Perfect Human Mark 2" kind of thing. It's the perfect pattern for *you*, living *your* life. *You* put it together!

Reprogramming your Money-Mind

And what's more, you put it together with the idea that you would succeed. You didn't set yourself up for failure.

You planned your life to bring out the best in yourself. From that space of wisdom, before birth, you could see the brilliance and perfection of your bigger, spiritual self. You could see the deep reserves of strength and compassion you held within you. You planned your life in order to call out those inner strengths and to draw out more of the shining light within yourself. So that means that whatever kind of mess your life seems to have got itself into, there is always a way through. And the way to find that is to tune into your inner guidance.

Your guides and angels are constantly holding that vision of the highest and best version of you in the Light. They know just how strong and beautiful your spiritual self is and they want you to bring out that beauty in your life, even more than you do. Throughout your life, 24 hours a day, they are holding this vision of your highest potential, intending it into being. You have a tremendous team behind you! So let's see how you can tap into their help and advice more directly.

Opening to Guidance

Opening to guidance can start with tuning into intuition - your own inner wisdom.

How does intuition work?

Your mind is like an iceberg - most of it is below the surface. Your conscious mind can deal with 5-9 bits of information at once. Your subconscious mind can deal with perhaps 11 million bits of information at once! Which part of your mind is likely to have the best idea about what is going on? Your intuition is the result of the information processing that your subconscious mind is doing.

How do I turn it on?

To access your intuition, you need to turn down the volume on your left brain that talks at you in words - all the time, if you let it. The gabble from your left brain drowns out the quiet voice of your intuition. Then you need to drop into the word-less consciousness of your right brain - which is very good at accessing your intuition.

To tune into word-less consciousness, try these exercises:

1. **Scan through your body. Which part of your body is most relaxed right now? What is the feeling that lets you know**

you're relaxing? Where else can you find it happening now?
2. **Hold your hand in front of your face and close your eyes. Feel your hand from the inside - without moving it. Can you feel each finger from the inside? With your eyes still shut, can you touch your nose with your finger?**
3. **Focus on your heart and relax. With every breath, notice a loving feeling growing in your heart. Breathe in softness and warmth and gentleness to your heart and notice how it gets softer and warmer. This takes you right out of fear and anxiety. You feel safe.**

Ways to work with intuition

Make a decision and live with it
Make a definite decision and live with it for a week. So, for example, make a definite decision that you will retrain for a new job. What happens? How do you feel? What do you notice? What do you do differently?

Now make the other decision - definitely - and live with it for a week. So, using our previous example decide quite definitely that you will stay in your present job. What happens? How do you feel? What do you notice? What do you do differently? Now - which decision *feels* better?

Timeline it

(This works best if you can stay quite Word-less)
Stand up. Imagine you are standing at your decision cross roads and see your choices as branching paths ahead of you. Take one of the possible decisions and walk that path until you reach a point you feel is 6 months ahead. What do you notice?
Come back to your cross roads and do the same with the other path(s). Now come back to the cross roads and look at your decision point. Which path is brightest?

Working with Guides

Different people have different beliefs about guides. Some people think of them as Guardian Angels. Other people think of them as relatives who have passed on and now offer loving help and support from the other side. I have met people who believed that their guides were aliens from another galaxy who were much more spiritually evolved than humans. Other people think that guidance doesn't really come from external beings of any kind but from the wise parts of our own selves. In the end, who you think your guides are probably matters less than how you can get guidance from them!

Some people seem to consistently get guidance in dreams. You may not even remember dreaming, but just find you wake up with new clarity and knowing

Reprogramming your Money-Mind

what to do. It helps if you *ask* for guidance before you go to sleep.

For other people, guidance comes as coincidences. For example, 3 people tell you the same thing in one day or you pass a billboard that seems to tell you the answer to your question only 5 minutes after asking the Universe for help with finding an answer. Sometimes you keep reading the same information everywhere.

Some people use dowsing with a pendulum to ask *yes/no* questions. The pendulum swings one way for *yes* and another way for *no*. (Ask it first to show you which is which!)

Other people prefer to get answers in meditation. They visualise walking through a garden where they meet a wise person who talks to them. For this you need a bit of time, so that you can relax into a quiet state. Some people prefer to pray. They ask for help and then trust that they will be shown a solution. The most important bit of getting guidance is to *ask* for it! Trust that you are heard and that guidance will come.

If you're not sure whether or not you got a message right, ask your guides to make it really clear for you. They will repeat the message until you get it, if it's really guidance. Sometimes, the trick is to notice the guidance in the first place! if you ask for it, it will always come - somehow.

Asking your Higher Self for guidance

In our culture, we tend to treat spiritual practice a bit like a vending machine.

- Say these prayers and you'll be healed/get a job/ get what you want.
- Do this meditation practice and you'll accumulate merit/ be able to fly/ see God.
- Go on this pilgrimage and you'll be healed/ remove all your karma/whatever.

Just for today, listen instead of talking, receive what is offered instead of demanding. Just sit quietly and breathe until you feel still inside. Let yourself relax and let your breathing naturally slow down all by itself. Focus on your heart until you feel held in love. Then ask God/ Universe/ Higher Self/ Tao/ Whatever you call that Higher Power:

- What is *your* vision for my life?
- What is *your* plan for me?

Or bring to mind a problem you have - perhaps a decision you must make or a dilemma you face. Send your dilemma/problem/decision out from you, asking for guidance. And then let go. Stop worrying - let go of mulling it over and poking at it and sit again in quietness. Intend to feel into your Perfect Pattern and assess which solution fits best with it. Ask

Reprogramming your Money-Mind

yourself "What *wants* to happen in my life? How is my Perfect Pattern trying to show up in this situation? What's the best possible outcome that it's trying to bring about?"

Drop into the silence, deep in your heart. Just rest in the peace, knowing you are loved and that - whatever things may look like on the outside - all is well. Open up a loving, receptive space for guidance to come. It may come then, while you sit, or later, as you are going about your everyday life. Be on the alert for unusual conversations, inspiring books, and meaningful dreams - or just "inklings", hunches, ideas that come up over and over and don't seem to go away. You may find yourself called to something more than you have been asking - or just different.

Working with the ideas in this section can totally change your relationship to money. You can go from feeling that, somehow, all of life is against you to seeing life as a wonderful adventure designed to bring you more joy than you had ever believed possible. You can change from believing that going after money - even enough to keep your life ticking over on a very basic level - will take you away from your spiritual path, to seeing that opening to abundance on every level can be part of your spiritual growth and exploration and can deepen your connection to the Divine.

Wendy Aridela

The legacy of ancestral beliefs

Simply by looking at our lives, we are invited to ask ourselves, "What kinds of beliefs must I have to have created a world like this around me?" Bear in mind that some of these beliefs won't be conscious at all. We inherit patterns of beliefs from our families and our cultures that may go back for generations.

For example, in meditation, I've experienced deep ancestral belief patterns in me that seem to go back to my grandmothers who lived on the West Coast of Ireland in great poverty. I experienced weeping with the bitter regret of a long line of mothers, exhausted with frequent child-bearing and then losing too many of those children to the kinds of health problems made worse by cold, damp, malnutrition, and the smoky environment caused by open fires made from peat. I felt in myself their despair that there was never enough of anything to go round - not enough money, food, clothes, fuel - or love. I had no idea I was carrying these patterns from hundreds of years ago, but they were definitely there at some level of my subconscious mind.

On a much less esoteric level, I know that growing up in the 1950s, in post-war Britain, had a powerful effect, too. When I look at (colour!) photos of my childhood, it's apparent how drab everything was. So many people seem to be dressed in grey, beige, or other dull colours. School dinners appear in my

Reprogramming your Money-Mind

mind's eye as grey steamed fish, grey potatoes and grey watery cabbage, all slathered in grey parsley sauce and served on grey plates. Everything was in short supply. Following the war years and then the many years of continued rationing, everyone was still in the mindset of "Make Do and Mend."

My parents were very dysfunctional around money, with both of them in different ways coping with family legacies of poverty consciousness. But even if they hadn't been, it would have been difficult to grow up at that time, in those surroundings, with a happy confidence that "This is an abundant Universe," or that "All my needs are always met."

Whatever time you grew up in, it will have had its own blend of craziness around money, whether it was the over-the-top self-indulgence of the 1970s, the "I'm all right, Jack" get-rich-quick politics of the 1980s, the politically correct simplicity of the 1990s or the enforced austerity of the recent years after the Banking Crash. So, on top of any strange or limiting beliefs from your family or school, there's the weird and wonderful flavour of the age to take into account.

And all of this adds into the rich mix of what Jung called the "Collective Unconscious" - the field of beliefs, ideas and concepts about the world that shape whole civilisations.

Wendy Aridela

It's my belief that at this time when the values that have shaped society for a long time are being challenged as never before, and we seem to be going through a massive paradigm shift, there are many people who have chosen to be born at this time with a commitment to work through their ancestral beliefs about money, gender, health, religion, ethics, power, livelihood or our relationships with other living things and the planet itself.

I believe that there's the equivalent of a "spiritual clean-up squad" working on the collective unconscious, fetching some of these crazy old patterns out into the light of consciousness so that they can be released for ever. You may well be one of them, if you have ever had the sense that some of your Money-Stuff has been handed down through your family. By clearing out the old patterns around money from your family energy-legacy, you are also helping to clean out the Collective Unconscious and open all of humanity to more light, more love and more abundance. You're helping to shift the blocks that keep all of us from making the difference we could make and being all we could become.

Section 3
Reprogramming the Emotional Level

SECTION THREE - Reprogramming the emotional level

What this section is about

Living an abundant life obviously has a lot to do with how you feel. Even if you're a billionaire, your life is going to feel a whole lot less abundant if you are constantly plagued with shame, fear, guilt, doubt or anger.

The famous movie, "The Secret" that introduced so many people to the Law of Attraction ended with the instruction "Be Happy Now." (if you haven't discovered it, you can find out more here: [http://www.thesecret.tv/)](http://www.thesecret.tv/) Now, that is fantastic advice, but for many people, it's about as realistic as saying, "Fly to Jupiter now." How do you *be happy now*, if you feel angry and upset? How do you *be happy now* if you're afraid? How can you possibly *be happy now* if you're a victim of tragedy or your life is an unfolding catastrophe?

How is it possible to let go of the pain of the past? Is it possible to choose how you feel, even when circumstances are difficult? When other people are annoying, or terrifying, or simply stubbornly stupid, is it possible that I can still be happy? And *should* I be happy? When the world is in such a mess and so many people are suffering, is it OK to be glad? That's what this section is about.

Discovering Your Values

Why is it important to be clear about your own values? And what do values have to do with money? Well, more than you'd expect, as it turns out. If you are unclear about your values, it makes it harder for you to know what "having an abundant life" means to you. For each of us, living abundantly means having in our lives a whole lot more of what we value. But we don't all value the same things.

So, for example, if it's important to you that other people respect you and see you as successful, status symbols such as a luxury car or a large house may be genuinely important to you. You may work extremely hard over many years to get promoted to a position with prestige attached to it - CEO, partner, owner of your own company. You probably put quite a lot of importance on being well turned out - whether that's wearing an obvious designer suit or simply dressing with understated, quiet elegance. For you, life without these things wouldn't really be abundant. It might still be worthwhile. You might experience considerable job-satisfaction. But, for you, some of the abundance would be lacking.

One the other hand, status symbols might not be important to you at all. For you, what's important might be making a difference in the world. Even if someone gave you a diamond-encrusted Rolls-Royce, it wouldn't mean as much to you as stopping the oil companies who want to drill in the Arctic, or pushing through the legislation that brings in a fairer voting system, or creating a school in which children can be genuinely happy and fulfilled. Knowing your values gives you a compass to show you where *your* abundant life is to be found. In the simplest possible terms, we all want more of what we value. So, how do you discover what that is?

The Values cards

On the next few pages, you'll find a set of values cards. You can scan them into your computer and print them out or simply photocopy the pages. Alternatively, you can download them from my website, by copying the link here:

http://ow.ly/Uessl

Once you have printed them or copied them, cut them into separate cards. Each card shows a value. To find which ones are important to you, first of all go through the pile and discard all the ones that aren't particularly important. This will reduce the pile by quite a bit. Next, sort the remaining values into two piles, *Most Important* and *important - but not so crucial.*

Now, put the pile of Most Important values in order from most to least important. Try not to have ties. If you can't decide which of two values is more important, ask yourself, "If I had to pick A *or* B, which one would be more vital to my sense of integrity? Which one would I suffer most from letting go of? This won't necessarily be easy, but it can be enormously helpful. At the end of this exercise, you will be clear on what are your top values. The top 3-5 are probably the ones that will contribute most to your sense of abundance. They are the values that tell you what kinds of goals you need to pursue.

Now, the Reality Check! Would someone looking at your life from the outside be able to guess your values? Would they be able to clearly see what it is that you value? If so, then you can congratulate yourself. You have a truly abundant life! It may not yet contain all the money you would like it to have, but you are probably fairly happy and contented with it, nonetheless.

If not, what would other people see? Would they perceive your life to be a bit of a mess, as if you weren't really sure *what* you valued? Or would they see a life that might look fulfilled from *someone else's* idea of an abundant life, but is not very much in accordance with *your* values at all? If so, you may have been living someone else's dream. It may be your parents' vision of what they wanted you to become. It could be your partner's dream. Or it could be your own dream - but from an earlier time of your life.

VALUES CARDS 1	
Peace	Connection to Spirit
Freedom	Adventure
Variety	Prosperity
Achieving	Winning
Security	Joy
Meaning	Balance

VALUES CARDS 2	
Love	Creativity
Growing and Learning	Authenticity
Sustaining Relationships	Wellbeing
Excitement	Integrity
Contribution	Fame
Compassion	Respect

VALUES CARDS 3	
Recognition	Making a Difference
Influence	Autonomy
Family	Status
Care for the Planet	Wealth
Inspiration	Connection and Community
Generosity	Flow

You can download these cards at: *http://ow.ly/Uessl*

Reprogramming your Money-Mind

Your values aren't set in stone - they can change over time. Sometimes going through a major upheaval or a tragedy in your life can make you re-evaluate things on a deep level and bring about a big values shift. Someone dies. Or someone is born. You lose your job or your money or your reputation. Or you get promoted, become famous, inherit millions. Whatever the trigger is, something shifts and you realise that you've outgrown your old self. Your values are different. On some level, you're a different person from who you used to be. And what you need in order to feel that your life is truly abundant has shifted too.

So it's important to stay up to date with your values, because going after goals that are in conflict with the values you hold right now will, sooner or later, cause you to sabotage your own success. On some deep level, you recognise that you are selling yourself short. Whenever you put energy into what you don't really want, not only do you get more of it, but you go without the people, things and opportunities that would truly make your life feel worthwhile. There's not enough time or energy in your life to pursue two sets of conflicting goals.

You need to stay focused on the values that are most closely tied in with your sense of what it takes to feel abundant. For example, honesty and integrity are important for most people to feel that their lives are rich and fruitful. It must be hard to feel good about the wonderful life you have, if you achieved it by selling crack cocaine to high school students. (Or anyone else!) Or you made your money from gun-running or from pimping prostitutes.

Clearly, I am picking extreme examples here, to make a point - but you most certainly don't have to be a law-breaker to feel that you are living out of alignment with your deepest values. The "mid-life crisis" made famous in endless films and TV shows is often about the wake-up call that happens to people in mid-life if they've been following someone else's dreams for them. Or else the TV shows are about people who pursue the goals that society told them were most valuable - fame, money, status - and then discover that, without love, family, connection, community and real contribution, they end up wealthy, famous and glamorous but also immensely sad and meaningless.

Some questions to ask yourself

1. Which are my most important values?
2. On a scale of 1-10, how closely am I living in alignment with my values?
3. In which areas of life do I live closest to my values?
4. In which areas of life do I miss the mark most widely? Where am I most out of alignment with my values?

5. Would my values be obvious to someone who looked at my life from the outside? Would they show up in what I do as well as in what I say?
6. How can I improve my values-alignment?

Wendy Aridela

The Value of Generosity

Sooner or later, most books, programs or courses on Money, Abundance or Prosperity are going to mention generosity as an important value. This is often in the context of encouraging you to give, in order to receive back. A common response to this, especially initially, is an immense cynicism. "Of course these guys are encouraging me to give," you think. "They want me to give them my money! How convenient it is, that the way to get more money flowing in *to me* is to give more *to them*! Ha! Do they think I was born yesterday?" How do I know that some people respond like this? Because I used to be one of them!

Relax! I am not asking you for your money. But perhaps all these people do have a point, other than to simply line their own pockets? Could there be something in what they say? Let's have a look at the whole, vexed area of generosity.

If you forget the whole idea of giving-in-order-to-receive, which is not genuine generosity, anyway, what makes you feel generous? What inspires you to give away some of your money, some of your time or some of your possessions? Why is it that, following every disaster, millions and millions of pounds flow in to the disaster relief agencies, from ordinary people, just like you and me? Have you ever watched an appeal on TV for clean water for

Africa or for refugees, displaced by war and camping in deplorable conditions, and texted a donation on your phone, without even really thinking about it? What makes us do it? We don't know these people and we'll never see the results of our donations. But our heart is moved. We feel pity, compassion, a real desire to reach out and help.

No matter how little we may normally consider ourselves to have, we see in that moment that - compared with the victims of flood, earthquake or war - we are wealthy people. We have so much more than they have. We give to them, in that moment, not from a sense of obligation or from an idea that if we give, we'll get something back, but from generosity.

That's the value in genuine generosity - in giving freely, from the heart, we see ourselves as having plenty - enough to give some away. We start to change our belief that we are poor people, people who lack, people who don't have enough. We become wealthier in our own eyes. We change our perception of who we are.

Do you remember what I wrote in the last section, about the Law of Attraction? Our world is always a reflection of who we think we are. If we change our perception of ourselves, we change the world that is reflected back to us. How do you think your world is likely to change, if you start to see yourself as a person who has enough to give away some of it from simple open-heartedness? How do you think your world might change if you start to see yourself as wealthy enough to be generous? The world will always mirror your beliefs about yourself - so you will start to have more to give away!

And going back to the idea that the Law of Attraction responds to who you are rather than what you think, seeing yourself as a person who has enough to give some of it away is one of the most powerful shifts you can make. It brings you into very strong alignment with the more prosperous versions of you that are wanting to emerge.

Working with Jealousy and Envy

On the other hand, it's really important to work on any feelings you have of jealousy or envy of the abundance you see other people having. This is because jealousy and envy both come from a perception of lack. When you're experiencing them, you're seeing yourself as a victim, someone who's badly-done-to, someone who gets less than they should. Both jealousy and envy reflect an underlying belief that there's not enough to go round, so, if someone else has more, it means that there is less left for you.

Can you see how this is going to warp what can come in to you? Do you understand enough of the Law of Attraction now to realise that if you are focusing on "There isn't enough to go round," in any way, then that's exactly what you'll see more of, reflected in your world. However, I know from personal experience that letting go of jealousy and envy can be difficult. So which methods help?

Flower essences can be really helpful. Bach Flower essences are the easiest ones to find as they are on sale in health food shops and even some larger pharmacies. The most helpful ones may be WILLOW, which is the remedy for resentment and HOLLY, which is the remedy for anger as these are often the underlying emotions behind jealousy.

If you're prepared to shop around a bit and look online, I personally recommend Crystal Herbs. (I don't get commission for recommending them - I just genuinely think their essences are really helpful and speak purely as a satisfied customer.) You can find them here:
http://www.crystalherbs.com/selfhelp/abundance.asp

Stopping Complaining

If you genuinely want more prosperity in your life, complaining is a bad habit to be on the look-out for. Are you aware how much you complain? Most people are astonished when they start to take notice of just how many times a day they are moaning, bitching, griping, sneering, being disparaging, or otherwise complaining about their life!

Do you realise how much energy all of that is using up? And that's all energy that could have been used instead towards creating something better! It's energy that could have been used in noticing and responding to opportunities. It's energy that could have been spent creatively, writing, gardening, knitting, painting, baking. You could have been using that energy to create products to sell, talking to customers, or simply to make a better life for yourself by decorating the house, getting fit, cooking a delicious meal or even making new friends. But, instead, you were complaining.

If you're prepared to turn this habit around, try wearing a (fairly loose) rubber band on one wrist. Every time you catch yourself complaining, even in a jokey kind of way, swap the bracelet to the other wrist. This simple exercise has far-reaching effects - you'll be amazed at how much it can shift your outlook! See if you can go without complaining for 21 days. If you can, you will be a changed person at the end of it.

If you'd like to make this a longer term project - or get other people you know on-board, too - you may be interested in the worldwide movement for a Complaint-Free World. You can find out more at: *http://www.complaintfreeworld.biz/*

Working with Wanting

We all know that "wanting" is not spiritual. We know that desires will get you stuck in chasing after stuff that - in the long run - won't make you happy. But what's the alternative?

Traditional religion - of many kinds - suggests that we train ourselves to let go of desires. Nuns, monks and hermits take vows of poverty, owning only the clothes on their back sometimes. It seems that the alternative to "wanting" is going without - to reconciling yourself to never having, to a life of quiet (but very spiritual!) resignation, For years, I tried to live like this. The snag with it is that - despite renouncing want - you are living in a sense of lack. Holy lack, maybe. Very spiritual poverty. But the lack and the poverty are the root of your experience. Recently, I've seen another alternative.

The way to not-want is not to "stuff" all of your wanting into some dark closet of the mind, and to become resigned. It's to celebrate having. It's to *know* that I am totally loved, that all my needs are met and that I live in an utterly abundant world. I understand that the wellspring of that abundance is within me and is inexhaustible.

Not only that, but if I start to trust that - whether or not I actually get what I want - going after desires, or deciding not to go after them, will teach me something, then I can stop being afraid of having desires come up. Some of them are - after all - useful indicators of what I need (or what I think I need!) to keep me well and happy.

A lot of the discomfort with wanting is in the contrast between feeling the desire for what you want, and feeling the fear, or even despair, that you will never have it. I've discovered that it's possible to have the desire without the fear. Just as when you were a little child, there were times when you *knew* you were going to get what you wanted - Mom and Dad had *promised* you a bike for your birthday, or you were *certain* that Santa would bring you the roller skates - we've all experienced times when there was something quite enjoyable in the anticipation of wanting something, once you could be reasonably certain it was on its way.

Well, once you trust the Universe on a deep level, you can be sure that at least the essence of what you want is on its way. Maybe not in exactly the way you have imagined it, but something is coming that will give you the same feeling and tick the same boxes. And if not that, then something better.

You may have to do some work on yourself first, to become more of the kind of person to whom this thing that you want would flow naturally. You may have to take some inspired action in the world. But you don't have to be afraid of your desires, because

Reprogramming your Money-Mind

you can relax into seeing how the path towards what you want simply opens before you, step-by-step.

When I begin to trust that, because I am totally held in the hands of love, all things in my life - no matter how difficult-seeming - carry the seeds of my greatest good, then I can relax into trust and radiant gratitude. All of my good is blossoming in my life. I live in a sense of gratitude and security. I'm not plagued by wanting because I am filled with plenty, with having, with rejoicing in the incredible richness and unceasing generosity of life. Maybe spiritual people should start to take a vow of plenty?

Wendy Aridela

Forgiveness - the big step forwards

When you saw this section heading, you may well have wondered what on Earth forgiveness has to do with money? The answer lies in the amount of energy you use up in not forgiving. Whether you are holding a grudge, or holding on to resentment, or holding onto a sense of having been wronged in some way, you are holding on. The language you use emphasises that. Just imagine that - that you are holding your grudge or your pain in your hands.

Now, imagine holding out your hands to receive. You can't do it - because at least one of your hands is being used to hold on to whatever you're holding onto! I understand, of course, that this isn't literally happening, but it is happening at an energy level. As long as you are holding onto any kind of pain from the past, you can't be fully open to receive. And if you're holding onto lots of things, you may be barely open at all to receive good things in the here-and-now.

This is not to condone the harm that was done to you or to deny your pain. Forgiveness is not about pretending that everything from the past doesn't matter any more or coming up with nice-sounding excuses such as, "I understand that they didn't really know what they were doing." No! Forgiveness is not about letting the other person off the hook. They have done what they have done and life itself will, in due course, bring them the consequences of that.

Forgiveness is about letting *you* off the hook. Forgiveness is about allowing yourself to put down the burdens of the past and to make a new start in life. It's about allowing yourself to finally let go of the pain, grief, shame and regret and to move forwards into life.

I'm not pretending for one moment that this is easy. You may need professional help from a counsellor or therapist if you have had some really difficult experiences. But forgiveness is something you owe to yourself, in order to be able to live life with joy again. You can't really experience living abundantly on any level until you do.

In the end, forgiveness is a decision you make - that you have had *enough* of seeing yourself as a Victim, of feeling damaged, disempowered, angry, hurt and humiliated. Yes, the past happened and maybe life can never be the same again, but that Perfect Pattern for your life is still in every cell of your body. There *is* a way forward, a way to grow and learn, a way to release the pain and to know joy again. You may not yet know what it is, but it is there, somewhere, because in the end, *nothing* can separate you from your good.

Wendy Aridela

That light that you are is still inside you. Nothing can dim it or put it out. You can choose to take back your power, to know yourself as a good and powerful person, despite everything that has happened. Look around you - there are so many empowering examples.

One person whose story I have personally found very inspiring is Nick Vujicic. You can find out more about him from some of the videos he has on YouTube, here: https://www.youtube.com/user/NickVujicicTV Nick Vujicic was born without arms or legs, but has become a motivational speaker who reaches out to all kinds of people with a message of hope.

He is not the only one. Great examples are everywhere. There are people who have managed to make their peace with incest, torture, rape, disability from war or accidents, and even the deaths of their children. It's not that they feel no pain now. It's not that they think that what happened to them was OK. It's that they have made the decision to be bigger than their pain - to not let their pain define all that they are, or can be, as human beings.

Again, please don't think I am saying that this is easily done or that I am in any way blaming you if you have something in your past which you find it hard to forgive. I'm simply saying that making the decision to *move towards* forgiveness - even if you can't quite do it yet - is one of the most empowering things you can do for yourself. It makes so much difference to your life. As I said earlier, I recognise that, if your past holds serious problems, you may need professional help. But for many of us, there is a lot we can do ourselves, to let go of the many smaller hurts and grudges we are burdening ourselves with.

Releasing the pain of the past

Write it down; let it go - For this, you only need a pen and paper. (You can do this on computer, but I think it helps you let go more dramatically to do it by hand.) Just write down everything that happened and all your pain, shame, anger, fury, humiliation or shame that you feel as a result. Swear. Curse. Weep. Let go of the whole lot.

Write until you can't write any more, until you feel you've either got it all out of your system or that you've done all you can for now. Read it through when you've finished. Allow yourself to fully feel all the emotion that is tied to this. Now, tear up the paper into tiny pieces - no bigger than centimetre squares. Rip it into shreds. And feel as you do so that you are finally tearing up this story from your past - you are destroying it and its power over you.

Now, either flush the bits of paper down the toilet or throw them into a fast-flowing river. Watch the water swirling them away. Feel the relief of seeing them go, for good. Or - if you have elderly plumbing - take the paper outside and set fire to it. Watch it burn to blackened ash. Feel the flames devouring your pain, destroying the story, freeing you from it.

Some people may find they need to do this two or three times, but each time you do it, the emotional tie to your past gets weaker and weaker until you can truly feel you have let it go.

Cutting the ties that bind - If the pain you want to let go of is tied up with a conflicted relationship, then I really recommend you read the book by Phyllis Krystal called "Cutting the Ties that Bind - growing up and moving on." You can find it on Amazon, here: http://ow.ly/UPFSd (I don't get commission for recommending this book - I recommend it because I have personally found it very helpful in the past.)

In it, she describes a powerful visualisation exercise in which you imagine the bonds between you and the other person as ties between you, which you then cut. Done properly, as described in the book, the process is amazingly powerful - I felt an instantaneous shift, releasing me from a painful relationship when I did it.

Flower essences - Most ranges of flower essences contain one for letting go of the past or for moving you towards forgiveness. The one I am most familiar with is the Bach flower essence, WALNUT. You can buy it from Health food shops and some larger pharmacies. It helps you to break links with the past, so that you can release hurt and pain and walk free.

Kindness meditation - This may not be easy, but it is extremely powerful. This is a simplified version of a traditional Buddhist meditation, called Metta-Bhavana
1. Think of someone you really love - someone who makes you feel all soft and warm, just thinking about them.
2. Hold that person in your awareness, and imagine waves of love pouring towards them from your heart. Sit until you can feel this strongly.
3. Now bring to mind someone who you are fairly neutral about - a work colleague, perhaps, or a neighbour
4. Hold that person in your awareness, just as you did for the previous one, and imagine waves of love pouring towards them from your heart. Again, sit until you feel this strongly.
5. Now bring to mind someone with whom you have had problems. It could be a recent problem or an old one from way back.
6. Hold that person in your awareness, just as you did for the previous one, and imagine waves of love pouring towards them from your heart. Again, sit until you feel this strongly. You may not be able to do this, at first. You may find this brings up a lot of emotion, but breathe through it, and keep intending to pour out love. If this is a big hurt from your past ,

you may not feel love the first time (or even for a long time) but just do the best you can.

7. Now hold yourself in your awareness, as if you were looking at someone else.

8. Let love pour from your heart to you. (Some people find this bit hardest of all.)

This is not an easy meditation for many people - but the effects can be far-reaching. You can let go of old pain that has been hurting for years, and experience that you can finally forgive someone and let them go. Take it at your own pace and go easy on yourself, especially if your past has some difficult stuff in it. If you really feel ready to let go and heal, this can help.

After forgiveness, what then?

If you have defined yourself by a big hurt in your past - I'm an incest survivor, or I am recovering from domestic violence, for example - life can feel very strange once you have started working on forgiveness. There can be a sense that you don't know who you are any more. You can almost find yourself grieving for the version of you that you are letting go of.

Be gentle with yourself and allow the process to take time. Get all the help and support you need, whether from friends and family or from professionals. Prayer or meditation will help. Reach out to your guides and angels. And trust that the day will come when, Like a rainbow after a storm, the sun breaks through and you begin to open to a new life with greater freedom and wider horizons.

Wendy Aridela

Letting Go of Stress

You have only got to read a few books or articles about the Law of Attraction to get the idea that how you feel makes a difference to the kinds of people, events and opportunities that you seem to draw to yourself. You know this for certain if you've ever had "one of those days."

I'm sure you know the kind of day I mean. The alarm doesn't go off so you suddenly wake up with a start and realise that it's late, late, *late!* Aaargh! You leap out of bed and put your bare foot into cold vomit, left by your cat, who has been sick on your bedside rug overnight. The car won't start, the train is late, you remember you left your packed lunch on the sideboard only once you're 10 minutes from home and the day goes downhill from there. It's non-stop, one thing after another. We've all had days like this. It seems as if there's nothing left that *could* go wrong but hey, here's one more thing.....

On days like this, it's easy to spot that the more wound-up you get and the more you're anticipating the worst, the more bad things happen. Sometimes it takes going to sleep to break the cycle.

On the other hand, most have us have also had at least the occasional blessed-by-Heaven kind of day when it seems as if nothing can go wrong. Everyday life seems to turn into something like Tai Chi. You pour the water from the kettle into your mug and turn back just in time to take the hot milk off the stove to go into your coffee. The toast pops up just as your eggs are perfectly cooked and as you sit eating breakfast, the sun is pouring in through your window and the garden is filled with the sound of birdsong.

You're filled with gratitude for even the tiny everyday things - a flower growing between the paving slabs, the smell of fresh bread from the supermarket, the smile of a stranger - and you have a perfect day.

You're in the right place at the right time, all day long. Someone tells you the exact piece of information you needed to complete a project. You meet an old friend and find out about a wonderful opportunity. You reach the cafeteria just as the queue vanishes. Every traffic light turns green as you reach it. It's like having a charmed life. And at that time it's very obvious that the happier and more grateful you feel, the better life gets.

Putting yourself in the driver's seat

But this is the real world, right? Days like this can be as rare as hens' teeth. Most of life just happens. It's not up to you. No matter how happy and joyful you may feel, that annoying colleague you sit next to at work will *still* whistle through his teeth whenever he's reading his emails. The woman opposite you on the train will *still* sniffle and sniff with her head-cold, for the entire journey, instead of blowing her nose. The person in the car in front of you will *still* drive at 28mph - even though this is a 40mph zone. You can't do anything about them, can you? Some things just make you fed up, annoyed, upset.... even totally freaked out. There's just nothing you can do about it, right?

Wrong! You maybe can't stop people around you doing all the things they do - but you can choose whether or not you allow them to spoil your day. The English language is quite deceptive. We say things like, "He makes me *so cross* when he does that," or "She makes me *livid* when she says things like that," and it sounds as if what we're feeling is caused by someone else. But it isn't, you know. It's caused by us. Other people do whatever they do. But how we respond depends on what we say to ourselves about what they're doing.

You can easily prove this for yourself. When you're having a good day, that annoying colleague, Phil, can whistle tunelessly through his teeth all he likes and you just shrug and think "Good grief! What an idiot! I'm so glad I'm not *married* to him!" Then you smile, and get on with your day, perhaps taking a moment to feel sorry for Phil's wife.

On a bad day, he doesn't even have to be in the room to annoy you. You start talking about him to your friend, and you can feel your blood starting to boil. "Have I told you about Phil?" you ask your friend. "He's this guy I work with. Annoying? - he could win Olympic Gold Medals for being annoying! He whistles tunelessly through his teeth all of the blasted time he's reading his emails! Good grief! He drives me *mental*!"

Now think about it - Phil is not even in the same room as you at this time. You're quite possibly not even at work. It may be the weekend. You haven't even set eyes upon Phil for at least 24 hours. He could be asleep in bed right now. He's not doing anything, anywhere near you. He's not there! And yet, you're furious. Can you see? *Phil is not the problem!* You are! The problem is what you think about Phil, what you feel about Phil, what you're saying to yourself about Phil - and you have the power to change that.

You can't change Phil. But you have an almost unlimited capability to change yourself and how you respond. Don't let Phil and the many other people like him dictate your day - put yourself in your own driver's seat. Make a decision that, come what may, you are drawing a line in the sand today. From now on, *you* get to decide how you feel - not the other people in your life. From now on, you're taking back your life. (I'll talk about how you can do that a few pages from now.)

Congratulations! You've just taken an enormous step closer to being happy now! And the more you feel positive about life, the more positive people, events and opportunities - including money - you'll draw into your life.

Dealing with Fear

There's a lot to be afraid of in life, it seems. Come to that, quite a lot of those fears are connected with money. What if you don't have enough? What if you do have enough, but you lose it? What if you get swindled? What if you lose everything? What if you lose your job and then you haven't got enough money?

What if you make a lot - but then lose half your friends? What if you make a lot and then suspect a lot of people are only making friends with you because of the money? How could you tell who *really* likes you? What if you win the Lottery? How will you cope with the stress? (Ok, so maybe that's a stress you wouldn't mind experiencing!)

Fear and family stories

But seriously, most people have a lot of fears around money - and those fears often stand in the way of having more. For example, many people subconsciously stop themselves from earning more than their parents. This may be from a feeling that somehow, to earn more than they do would be disrespectful. Maybe it would send them a message that you think you're better than them? Perhaps it could even be taken as you criticising them for not doing as well for you as you are now doing for your family? It may not be your parents you're subconsciously measuring yourself against - it could be a brother or sister or cousin - even a friend. Is there someone in your life it wouldn't feel good to you to be doing better than?

Do you feel disloyal to your family if you get promoted above a certain level? Did you get told as a child that "People like us never do XYZ?" or "No-one from our family would ever be like that/ do that/ work in a job like that?" It can be hard to go against strong family messages like that, because on some level, those messages have been part of our identity for much of our life. Even if we're now happy to move on - and our family members are actually as proud of us as can be, there can still be a lingering sense that it's somehow not *right* to take this next step, get promoted to this next level, or go after this bigger-than-usual deal.

Fear of loss, lack and going without

For most people, of course, their greatest fear around money is of losing it or of there not being enough to go round. This is magnified by the media who know that bad news sells papers and TV programmes. So we are bombarded with stories of banks collapsing, whole countries whose economy goes under, people whose businesses go bust, famous people and the not-so-famous who go from having-it-all to having nothing.

We're constantly exposed to advertisements that ask us what we'd do if we contacted a fatal illness, how our families would cope if we died, or how we'd even pay for our funeral. Injury lawyers keep telling us that tragic accidents happen all the time and that only skilled legal intervention will get us a fair amount of compensation.

Crime watch programmes tell us about frightening people who commit robberies, hold up banks, mug innocent citizens and break into houses to steal anything beautiful and valuable. (Especially from homes without expensive alarm systems and from people without adequate insurance!) We're constantly told that we live in a dangerous world. Be afraid! Be very afraid! (Cue spooky music!)

In reality, we live in a vastly safer world than our grandparents did. Go to any railway museum or canal museum and you are sure to read of disasters that killed dozens of the men who worked to build those transport systems in the 18th and 19th centuries. There were accidents with explosives, floods, collapsing bridges, fires, landslides, and cave-ins. The navvies died of wounds, fevers, and infectious disease causes by inadequate sanitation.

These days, accidents at work still happen - but thanks to safety legislation, they are very much rarer than they used to be. Victims of accidents receive the kind of excellent medical care our grandparents could not have imagined and can usually expect compensation.

In the same way, the days when anyone undertaking a journey from one city to the next had to worry about highway-men are long gone - at least for most of us in the Western world. Yes, robbers, thieves and burglars still exist - but they aren't the real fear to most of us that they were to our ancestors, living in towns with no street lighting, no police force, and no telephones.

A friend of ours was recently a victim of credit card fraud. Her card was copied and the thieves had attempted to buy a lot of goods with it. What was the result? The thieves were caught. The banks cancelled the credit card. Our friend had several days of stress and inconvenience. She got quite upset. She had to go and spend an hour or so at the bank to sort it all out. She spent several days without a credit card. But that was it. The bank refunded all her money and gave her a new credit card. It's nasty. But it's a long way from being held up at blunderbuss point by a highway-man and losing all your valuables and possessions that you have with you, followed quite possibly by being raped and shot.

Wendy Aridela

I'm not saying that all your fears around money are ridiculous. You may have some very real challenges in your life. But, whatever the challenges or problems, fear is almost definitely not helping. There's a very helpful saying:

"Can you do something about your problem?
If so, don't worry - just do what you can do.
If not, don't worry, just do what you can do.
And if you can't do anything, relax - and don't worry!"

It's important to get your fears into perspective. For a start, stop listening to the news and reading the papers because their viewpoints are very unlikely to be helping!

Ask yourself what is the very worst that could happen. How would you cope with that, really? Yes, it would doubtless be horrible. Yes, you might experience stress, shame, and guilt. But you'd survive. You'd find a way through. How do I know? Because you always have found a way through - or you wouldn't be reading this! You'd be dead. Or in a psychiatric establishment. Or in prison.

So take back your power. Get professional help if you need it to help you sort out your finances and other life problems. Draw up a plan of action to start moving you from where you are today towards where you would prefer to be. Face the fear and refuse to let it have any more power over you.

Remember, if you hit the bottom, the only way out is up!

How to cope with Fear - practical strategies

We all experience fear from time to time. In small amounts, it's useful – it warns us to take care here. But in large amounts it can become overwhelming. So are there ways to avoid it, minimise it, or deal with it? Yes - and all 3 strategies can be appropriate at different times.

Avoiding fear

Sometimes you may be feeling fear for no good reason. There's actually no danger facing you right at this moment - you're just feeling an immobilising level of anxiety. At times like this, it's best to *avoid* fear – so how can you turn it off?

1. When the body is dehydrated, we are hard-wired to feel anxious. It's a stimulus to go and find water. Most people have lost touch with this but it is astonishingly effective. So drinking water can turn off unnecessary anxiety.

2. Eating lots of sugar can destabilise your blood sugar levels which creates feelings of shakiness and panic, for no good reason. Eating sugar also stimulates your adrenal glands to produce more adrenalin, making you feel wired and wound-up. It's hard to believe how much

of a difference cutting out - or cutting down on - sugar makes, until you try it.

3. Deep breathing is also very helpful. The feeling of fear is almost identical – physiologically – with the feeling of excitement. Fear is excitement minus the breathing – so breathe! Deeper breathing oxygenates your brain and removes panic, enabling you to think more resourcefully.

Minimising fear

Sometimes you may be feeling fear that is not totally imaginary – there really is some kind of problem. It's not life-threatening, so you don't need to run away or take urgent action. What you need is to be able to think clearly to solve a problem. The fear you are feeling isn't helpful. At times like this, it's best to *minimise* your fear. These suggestions may help.

1. Move! Fear is accompanied by a surge of adrenalin to enable you to run away from sabre-toothed tigers or whatever. Any vigorous movement will burn this off, leaving you feeling more grounded and in control – so run, jump, clean the car or dance like a loon for 5 minutes!

2. Rebalance yourself - Bach Flower Remedies enable you to rebalance yourself. MIMULUS helps when you are feeling a specific fear.

ASPEN helps when you feel vague ongoing anxiety.

3. Eat for Calm - At times when you feel afraid, it's tempting to eat lots of chocolate and sweets – comfort food. If, instead, you eat lots of greens, you build up your Magnesium levels which makes you feel calmer and more relaxed.

4. Meditate - Breathing into your Solar plexus will help to rebalance it and will always help to reduce or remove feelings of fear. You may find it helpful to imagine breathing in Olive green or Gold light.

Take action

Sometimes you may be feeling fear for a good reason. There really is a problem that you need to deal with. In that case, your best strategy is to *take action* – but not any action. Running about like a headless chicken is a tempting option, but is unlikely to be your best bet!

1. Before you take action, get clear about what you want your outcome to be. What do you want at the end of all this? This stops you rushing off in an unhelpful direction.

2. Do the vital stuff first. Is everyone breathing? Is someone bleeding? Are you going to lose your home? Sort out the big stuff!

3. Deal with now! If you try to sort out everything that will unfold over the next few days and weeks it's too much. Just fix what you can deal with *now!*

4. In whatever way it feels OK to you, get in touch with the sense that you can tap into guidance and support from other levels. So pray, meditate, do affirmations or a card-spread - anything that reconnects you with feeling supported from within.

5. This is not a time for being the strong-silent-type! Get help and support from others. Don't be afraid to ask – many people will say *yes.*

The more strategies you have, the less you need to be fearful about feeling fear!

Mastering your mood - how to feel good more of the time

I'm hoping that, by now, you are starting to feel that you are not so much at the mercy of outside events as you have previously thought. You can feel happy - or at least calm and reasonably resourceful - even when difficult things are happening. That advice to "*be happy now*" is seeming a bit more possible! You're beginning to believe that you could master some of the negative emotions that hold your good at arm's length. So let's give you even more strategies - it gets better!

Laughing and Smiling - your secret weapons

Most of us believe that we smile because we feel happy and laugh because something on the outside makes do so. But medical and psychological research into laughing and smiling has come up with some strangely counter-intuitive findings. It turns out that smiling can *make us* feel happy, even when we were pretending to begin with.

When you smile, your brain produces all kinds of feel-good chemicals that make you feel happy. It's almost impossible to smile and feel stressed at the same time. Try it! Right now! Smile! Let your face relax so that your smile isn't tight and forced. Let go and relax into the smile, so that your eyes start to twinkle. Just smile - and notice how, straight away, there's a little lift in your mood. Even if it's not a very good smile, maybe a bit wobbly round the edges or still a bit forced, it has a positive effect. Take a moment, right now, and notice the little changes it has caused. What did you notice? The more you do this, the more powerful it gets, because you get better at it!

Now, if just a teeny little smile can lift your mood, what could a really good belly-laugh do for you? When you were a child, you probably laughed all the time - research has found that the average 2-year old laughs 20 times a day. When was the last time *you* laughed 20 times in a day? If you're like most Westerners, you won't be able to think of an occasion in the last few weeks or even months. This can be fixed!

Laughter yoga was invented by an Indian doctor, Doctor Madan Kataria, who knew that laughter produces all kinds of beneficial changes in the body. It helps you heal, helps boost your immune system and helps you to counteract stress, for starters. Any drug that did all that would be flying off the pharmacy shelves!

Dr Kataria discovered that people could quite easily learn to laugh for no reason. You don't need to hear jokes or funny stories. Nobody needs to tickle you. You don't need to see a clown fall into a vat of custard. You can simply laugh, for no reason at all. If you want to explore this, go onto YouTube and put in "laughter yoga" as a search term. You'll get all kinds of examples.

I particularly liked this one: <ins>https://www.youtube.com/watch?v=_9OHtirEZM8</ins> which takes 20 minutes but there are lots, ranging from a few minutes to half an hour or so. If you want a very short video to watch, I made one myself which you can find here: <ins>https://youtu.be/QoabmrgLcE8</ins>

Laughter yoga can change the way you feel about life because it overturns so many of our ideas about the way that things are supposed to happen. We have all these beliefs about what has to happen to make us laugh, and then suddenly, someone comes along and shows us that we can just laugh - for no reason. Wow! We try it, and it seems to be true - it seems to work.

So, could we be glad for no reason, just because we wanted to? Could we be grateful, even if we don't seem to have some of the things we'd like? Could we feel OK about our lives, even when things are difficult? Could we? Well, it's probably worth a try, isn't it? After all, if we were wrong about what it takes to make us laugh, what else might we have been wrong about?

Roaring and Groaning - releasing anger and frustration

What about anger? That can be a difficult emotion to simply let go of, because it's often backed up with high levels of adrenalin in our bloodstream. Simply "stuffing" the anger, shutting it off or pushing it out of awareness doesn't work well because the adrenalin continues to circulate, making us feel shaky and ungrounded or very tense and wired.

One solution is to take action, very literally. Run round the block. Jump up and down. Sweep the floor or clean some windows. Skip. Move furniture. Do something energetic - and preferably something useful that will add a glow of accomplishment to your day! What this does is to "burn off" the adrenalin and so de-fuse the anger.

Another solution is to roar or to groan. Both these are loud sounds and use the muscles in your diaphragm - the sheet of thick, strong muscle between your ribs and your belly. As this is exactly the area where a lot of previously "stuffed" anger seems to get stored, both these exercise are good for releasing it.

Groaning - This is easier if you're standing up. Breath in and then breath out, groaning loudly. Allow your body to move in any way that seems to be helpful. I find that when I'm groaning, my body wants to flop forwards somewhat, bending in half at the waist. But how you move is up to you. Simply focus on groaning, as loudly as you can. (Inside your car, parked in a parking lot is a good place for this as you're unlikely to be noticed!) Really make a noise. This may feel a bit weird or unnatural, but it's amazingly helpful in letting go of a whole day's worth of stress and frustration!

Roaring - this is even more effective for coping with anger and frustration than groaning! Simply take in a big breath and then roar like a lion, as loudly as you can. Grrrrr! Raaaaah! Now try to do it even louder! (Again, inside your parked car is a good place for this.) You'll be amazed how much this can lift your mood - you may even end up laughing at yourself!

Meditation - the Secret of Calm

There is a lot of unhelpful rubbish written about meditation, so that some people feel it's a mysterious and esoteric art with about as much practical usefulness as being able to crochet spiders' webs. But basically, meditation is something astonishingly simple - it's training your mind to focus on one thing at a time, instead of leaping all over the place like a box of frogs.

This is a much less stressful way to do things than trying to juggle lots of tasks at once or do one thing while thinking of three others. What you choose to focus on is up to you, but whatever you choose, start small. Focus for a minute or two - don't aim for 15-30 minutes to begin with, although you may decide you'd like to work up to that. But it's better to meditate for 3 minutes, 5 times a day and stay pretty focused each time, than to meditate for 15 minutes in one go and then to spend most of that time worrying about the gas bill. Here are some suggestions of appropriate things to focus on:

Looking - simply look at a natural object - a pebble off the beach, a crystal or a flower, for example. The aim here is not to replicate Superman's metal-melting heat-vision! Look in the fascinated way that babies look at things. You're aiming for open-eyed wonder rather than tight-jawed concentration. Or sit in a relaxed way watching the shadows move under a tree or the clouds move across the sky. Simply enjoy looking and noticing the beauty around you as if you'd never appreciated it before.

Listening - pay attention, right now, to the background noises where you are. What can you hear? Now, behind that, can you hear quieter sounds? And what about behind them? Just keep listening for the quieter sound and the quieter sound. Sometimes, you reach a space where you sense that behind all of the everyday sounds, there's a vast and deep silence that's rather wonderful. Can you hear it? If not, simply enjoy what you can hear, for as long as you like.

Reprogramming your Money-Mind

Feeling - tune into your body, just as you are, right now. Where does it feel most relaxed? Which part of you feels most comfortable, right now? Can you feel your feet on the floor? How much of each foot is touching the ground? Can you feel that, from the inside? Can you become aware of each toe, separately, felt from the inside? Focus on your body, allowing yourself to really feel all the parts of it you're not normally aware of.

Breathing - Notice your breathing. You don't have to do anything to it like speed it up or slow it down - simply notice. Are you breathing through your mouth or your nose, right now? Don't change it - just observe. Notice how relaxing it is, just to follow your breathing in and out. Notice how it tends to calm you down and helps you feel grounded and centred.

If a worry crops up or your mind starts to tell you a story, can you let it go and choose to return your focus to your breathing? No pressure - just experiment. Does counting your breaths help you stay focused or does it make you feel under pressure? (Count from 1-10 and then go back to 1 - this isn't an exercise in counting big numbers!)

Meditation can be gentle and playful. Use it as a tool. Which kinds of meditation make it easiest for you to relax and focus? There's no right answer. People are different from each other and you may find that you don't always feel the same. Sometimes it is easier to look, sometimes to listen. Sometimes it's relaxing to count your breaths and sometimes not. Simply enjoy the exploration!

If you'd like to explore meditation in more depth, I've written a beginner's guide. It's called 'How to Meditate - when you haven't a clue how to get started' and you can find it on Amazon here: *http://ow.ly/USNBt* It's also available - even more cheaply - as a Kindle.

Section 4
Reprogramming the Physical Level

SECTION FOUR - Reprogramming the physical level

What this Section is About

For many people, the physical level would be the obvious place to start sorting out problems with money. To them money is absolutely straightforward - it's all about what you earn compared with what you spend and what you save. Anything else is just woo-woo wooliness. Obviously, I don't agree and I've just taken about 40,000 words to tell you why not. What I have found is that money-problems turn out to be a tangle of unhelpful and disempowering beliefs, emotions that are tied up in the past, and in all kinds of spiritual beliefs about money, God and what life is all about. Different people need to heal on different levels.

But, that said, for some people, the problems are very much on the material level. Maybe you don't have enough money coming in and need to find new income streams. Or you've never got your head around budgeting or managing money with the minimum of stress. Perhaps you need to rethink saving or you need strategies for paying off debt. Or maybe you simply need more energy to cope with the material world while still feeling vital and resourceful? Perhaps, for you, the place to begin is with your diet - even though that doesn't immediately seem to have anything at all to do with money? This section helps you explore all of this.

Wendy Aridela

Getting Real with your money

Real like a rich person (really!)

A lot of self-help books that take a New Age approach to money, especially if they are based to any degree on the Law of Attraction, will advise you to "fake It until you make it." The idea is that, if you act like a wealthy person, you'll change how you see yourself and the world, break free from your limiting beliefs and start to attract wealth into your life. To my mind, there's a fatal flaw in this.

If you are reading this book, if you have had serious glitches in your Money-Programming, if you've spent much of your life battling money problems, how much idea do you have about how wealthy people act? Really? I'm not talking here about how characters from TV soap operas act, or how wealthy people are portrayed in the press. I'm talking about real-life, solidly wealthy people, and how they really act and feel around money.

I may be jumping to conclusions here, but my guess would be - not much. My guess would be that a lot of the people you know have their own flawed Money-Programming. Their Money-Mess not be exactly the same as yours, but it's my intuition that if you knew a whole bunch of people who were totally sane around money, you'd have just asked them for advice years ago, followed it, and started living like they did. By now, you'd be happily contented, solidly wealthy, utterly sane around money and have people asking *you* for advice about how you do it. The fact that you are reading this suggests that things are otherwise!

The big snag with advice like "fake it until you make it," is that it doesn't work if you're following a bad example. It doesn't work if you're trying to copy some half-baked idea about how rich people behave, rather than copying reality. It doesn't work at all if you're behaving like a character from a soap opera. They are already totally fake! Behaving like them is not going to bring real results. The trouble with the idea of "faking it" is that, if you have no real idea about how rich people live, you may simply go out and spend a lot of money that you don't have on the kinds of things you think rich people have. What you end up with as a result is a maxed-out credit card, rather than a bulging-at-the-seams bank account.

Yes, wealthy people may buy designer goods. They may eat at expensive restaurants. You may see them spending a lot of money. But they are like icebergs. What you see is very small, compared with what you don't see. So you see the flying first class. You see the haute couture outfit. But what you don't see is the whole out-of-sight mass of savings, investments, property portfolios, stocks and shares, and money in the bank - the underwater part of the iceberg - that's supporting the bit of the iceberg you do see.

What makes a wealthy person is not spending a lot of money - though they may do that. It's the solid sense of comfort and security around money - knowing that you've got it covered and that you can relax and enjoy your life. It's feeling in control around money. It's knowing that, even if you lost your money, you could make more because you know how to make money. It's living life the way you choose to live, rather than a life dictated by what you need to do for money. It's having a life where your money is in balance with everything else - with loving relationships, a close family, with beautiful surroundings, with making a positive difference in the world and with feeling at peace with yourself. Living like that is not something you can achieve by just maxing-out a few credit cards.

Fearless Finances

So how do you get to live a life like that? The first step is to get real with your money. This may not be advice you wanted to hear. After all, some bits of this book have been pretty woo-woo. I've been talking about working on your beliefs, feeling more joy, getting a better relationship with the Universe. All a bit la-la, and unthreatening. But, as I said in the beginning, scrambled Money-Programming is usually multi-levelled. Some of that is almost definitely going to be solidly "Real World." If your money's in a mess, you need to stop running and hiding and you need to sort it out.

Reprogramming your Money-Mind

Wealthy people do not live in fear of their finances. So, whatever you've been doing up until now, draw a mental line in the sand and commit to a new beginning. Commit to a new life of Fearless Finances. You'll cope. You'll survive. Remember the idea of the Perfect Pattern for your life? Whatever size of mess you've created, there's a way through it and out of it, somehow, somewhere.

To find that you may need some help. I'm not a debt counsellor, a financial advisor or an accountant. But there are plenty of people all around you who are. There are people whose life's work is to help other people sort out their money and plan for a more prosperous and better-managed future. There are people out there with a whole lifetime of expertise in sorting out debt, organising savings, and helping you to create a financial plan that works for you. Go and talk to them. This is not something you have to sort out alone, unless you feel happy doing that. If you're going to move towards being a genuinely wealthy person, the first step is getting solid foundations in place, starting right where you are.

Where are you? Tracking the money-flow

The first step, then, in creating some solid foundations is to know where you are now. How much money comes in every month? Where does it go? What are you spending it on? Remember, you can't change anything you're not even aware of, so the first step is becoming aware.

Whether you use a small notebook and a pen, an Excel spreadsheet on your computer or whether you keep a memo on your phone, track all your money for a month. Make a written note of every penny that comes in - whether it's your salary, a rebate of some sort, a win at Bingo, or a friend repaying you for a loan. Write it all down.

And track every single penny that goes out, especially the small amounts it's easy to miss - a bar of chocolate, a latte, a newspaper. It's important not to lie to yourself. If you just spent £10 on lottery tickets, don't write down £2. If you just bought your fourteenth chocolate bar today, don't ignore it and pretend it didn't happen. This is you being fearless. For this month, you're facing up to *everything*. Solid foundations have to be built on truth - they can't stand on anything else.

At the end of the month, you have the hard part. You need to add up all the figures and think about them. How much came in? How much went out? How much of what went out was rock-bottom, inescapable expenses such as mortgage/rent, gas, electricity or water rates? How much did all those "little things" add up to - the bars of chocolate, the beers, the lattes, the newspapers? How much did you spend on food? On transportation?

Now, looking at what you see in front of you, what seems like a sensible first step? I can't tell you what to do because I'm not you. I'm not living your life and I don't know your circumstances. But most people find that they are spending more than they thought in at least some areas of their life. Some of this may be inescapable. But some of it lies within your power to change. I can't tell you what decisions to make. But even if only one thing leaps out at you, and you see one area where you could do something to improve your situation, start there.

Remember the Chinese saying, "The journey of a thousand miles starts with one step." Take that first step. Then, when you see another step, take that. Just keep moving forwards. This is how you end up being somewhere else - moving away from where you are now, one step at a time. Just as the road to being old and wise starts with being young and foolish, the way to being wealthy starts from being not wealthy - and from making a plan to move away from that, starting now.

Your financial plan

As I said earlier, you may decide that you need some professional help to sort out your finances, particularly if they are in a fairly sizeable mess. But if you have a smaller-scale problem, one you feel quite confident about tacking yourself, you may find the planning template on page 164 useful. It's one I used for years. You can download a copy of this planner from here: *http://ow.ly/Uessl*

At least every 6 months, I updated the plan. This is important because your circumstances change all the time. Prices for petrol or car-tax may change because of a Budget. You may update your phone or broadband agreement and end up paying more - or less - each month. Your eating habits change with the seasons, so you may change what you spend on groceries. You may move house and have a totally different set of household bills and expenses. So revisit the planner at least every 6 months.

Work out a realistic budget for your monthly outgoings. It may be useful to plan for spending less on groceries and petrol (for example) than you do now, but it's not a good idea to plan for things being as tight as you can make them for a long period of time. There will always be a few unexpected expenses, so build in some slack to the system.

It's important to have the right mental attitude when you're doing this. You're not setting yourself up for a lifetime of Scrooge-like scrimping and saving. This isn't a path to misery! This is a path to empowerment. It's your route to feeling in control and having that genuine sense of comfort around money that truly wealthy people have.

Reprogramming your Money-Mind

Money Planner

Month:

HOUSE Rent/ Mortgage .... Phone/TV/ broadband ...... Electric .... Gas .... Council tax ...... Water .... Insurance......... Other **TOTAL** .... LIVING Housekeeping....... Car - petrol.......... Insurance............. Tax..................... Clothes............... Birthdays/Gifts Other **TOTAL** -------------------- GIVING **TOTAL** ----------------- SAVING 1 2 3 4 **TOTAL**	Regular Planned Outgoings House Living Giving Saving Other TOTAL .... INCOME	Month	One-off expenses to budget for	Income minus Outgoings	Disposable Income
		I look after money			

167

Once you've read the section on saving that's coming up in a few pages, I hope you'll begin to get excited about the new possibilities that open up for you as you begin to get your finances on a more solid, planned footing. You'll begin to see how this kind of planning is creating a path to genuinely being a wealthier person, without having to "fake it" at all.

Increasing Your Income

So, what should you do if after the money-tracking exercise above, the first step that leaps to mind is "I need to get more money coming in?" With some kinds of work this is not so problematic. If you are in sales, for example, you will earn more if you sell more. If you're in banking, you may get a bonus every time you sell a mortgage or insurance policy to a customer, or when you open new accounts. So if you need some extra cash, you can work harder at selling products. If you work in a factory or in retail, you may be able to earn overtime for working some additional shifts.

But what if you're in a job that brings you a fixed income? If you're a teacher, for example, you'll earn the same salary whether you work a 40-hour week, a 50-hour week or an 80-hour week. (I speak from experience, here!) And you can't take on additional teaching work outside your regular job because schools are only open Monday to Friday, during term-time. There *is* no Saturday teaching work you can do. Many other jobs are similar - you can't earn any additional money within your existing job. So what do you do? That's what we'll be looking at in this section.

Your Skills Audit

You almost certainly have lots of skills that could earn you money, even if you've never thought of them as a source of income.

I don't mean you should change your job or even start up a business. But just maybe get into the habit of saying *Yes* to more passing opportunities. All those little bits of money add up so why not put yourself forwards? if your work-mate is willing to pay you to fix his computer, and you enjoy doing that, accept the money and the job. If you hear a friend moaning that her new curtains are too long, and you enjoy sewing, offer to turn them up for her, for a price you both feel is fair. (If you can't agree on a fair price, let it go. She can pay a shop to do them, do them herself or leave them too long - it's not your problem. You could also offer to swap skills if there's something she could do for you that you really want done.)

To give you a clearer appreciation of just what a gifted individual you are, try completing the table on the next page. When you've done it, just take a minute or two to have a proper look at it. Once you put some thought into it, haven't you got a lot of skills? Far more than you usually think, I'd bet. This doesn't mean you are now obliged to start earning money in hundreds of different ways. But perhaps it could open your eyes to some new possibilities?

Reprogramming your Money-Mind

YOUR SKILLS AUDIT

Skill	I	Example	Your Skills
Unfulfilled Skills	....dream of using this	I would love to give public talks	
Unappreciated Skills	...don't usually notice this	I can spell well	
Undeveloped Skills	...could use this differently	I could use my aroma therapy skills to make my own soaps	
Under-exploited Skills	...use only on special occasions	I can ice wedding cakes	
Unloved Skills	...do this well but don't enjoy it	I'm a good teacher but hate schools	
Underused Skills	....could do more with this	If I write a blog, I could write a book	
Unadvertised Skills	... don't tell people about this	I'm an expert at Tantric Sex	
Undervalued Skills	...think "who'd be interested?"	I can knit	

Wendy Aridela

You may never have thought of using some of these skills to earn money. There will be some of them you wouldn't enjoy earning money from and some where what you would get paid for using this skill would really not be worth the time you'd have to put in. (For example, I can knit - but the rate of pay most people earn for knitting up garments is miniscule if you work it out on an hourly basis. So I keep knitting as a hobby, rather than as an income source.)

But with a bit of thought, as you keep adding skills to the table over the next few days as they occur to you, some possibilities may open up. What do people regularly ask for your help with, for example? Are you good with computers? A dab hand at wall-papering? Excellent at organising parties or church fetes?

What do you get compliments for? Do people rave about your home-made chutneys and pickles, tell you that you have a way with animals or children, or always call upon you to read the announcements at church or at team meetings because you have such a clear voice?

And what do you enjoy doing? What makes the hours slide away for you? Do you get hours of enjoyment creating scenery for your model railway or embroidering floor-coverings for your dolls' house? Do you lose track of time when you're on Facebook or Pinterest?

Reprogramming your Money-Mind

You would be amazed at what other people will pay you for - because what you love to do and what comes easily to you is a total chore for them, something they hate. Or simply something they find dull and boring. Ask yourself what you love to do that other people don't.

To give you some ideas - I love Maths and I love playing educational games with children. It's something I do from choice with my grandchildren. But it's also something I have turned into an income by doing after-school tutoring with kids who find it hard to learn Maths. I play Maths games with them to help them learn times tables, and revise number bonds. It's not the main source of my income, but it's a regular strand - getting paid for something that I enjoy.

I have a friend who has turned her love of social media into an income. She has helped small businesses and her local church to set up Facebook pages, Pinterest boards, Twitter accounts and Youtube channels and then to keep them updated. For her, it's like being paid to have fun - she couldn't believe that there were people on this planet who don't enjoy being on the internet and who find dealing with social media intimidating and off-putting.

Imagine her astonishment at discovering that there weren't just one or two of such people, but *hundreds and thousands* of people who hate being on the internet, hate being on Facebook, hate making videos and audios! And hate it to the point that they are more than happy to pay somebody else to do it for them. When you enjoy doing something, it can be hard to imagine that some other people don't enjoy it, find it hard or can't get their head around it at all.

I hate getting cold and wet, for example. For me, a rainy day is an invitation to stay indoors and write. Yet I have regularly seen a couple of local women who earn money from walking other people's dogs. They set off through the rain chatting animatedly, with half a dozen or so dogs pulling on their leashes, yelping with excitement at getting out for a walk on the wet grass of the local commons and footpaths. To me, it's a vision of Hell, to go tramping in the rain through wet grass, surrounded by excited dogs. Urgghhh! But the dog-walkers appear to love it! So think about it. What else might people pay you for?

Turning your expertise into money

It's not just what you can do that you turn into more money, but also what you know. What do you know about that other people might want to know? Don't overlook the obvious! I have a friend who runs an ironing business. As an advertisement for it she put some videos on YouTube, showing how to iron everyday garments such as shirts. Within a few weeks of posting her shirt-ironing video, it had had more than 8,000 hits. That's 8,000 people who don't know how to iron a shirt!

How many people do you think there are who don't know how to look after their pets, get their baby off to sleep, clean their household appliances or bake bread? And that's not even thinking about the kinds of information that enthusiasts are after - such as how to improve their golf, how to customise their car, or how to ice wedding cakes. Where are your areas of expertise? And how could you turn them into money?

Writing

If you can write, the obvious answer is to write a book. These days it's tremendously cheap and easy to write a book and self-publish it. You don't have to pay a local printer hundreds of pounds to print 2000 copies of your book, which then sit in your garage for the next 5 years. Nor do you have to persuade a major publisher to accept your manuscript and publish it for you.

Instead, you can simply upload a Word manuscript to an online self-publishing site, such as Amazon CreateSpace. Follow their online tutorials for formatting your book, use their templates to create a cover and within a short space of time your book can be for sale on Amazon. You can find out more here: *http://ow.ly/UWbyD*

If you have expertise in writing itself, you can also earn money by helping other people to turn their expertise into books. You might write the book for them or simply offer simple editing or proof-reading services.

Another possibility for writers is to write an entertaining and informative blog. If you get enough people following you for your tips on golf, healthy eating or whatever, you might also be able to earn money from hosting relevant advertisements. You can find more information on Google.

Audio tracks

If writing is not a great strength of yours, you could consider creating CDs or audio downloads. Many people listen to audio tracks in their car as they drive or via a smart-phone. This works well for information that doesn't need visuals to explain. For example, information about healthy eating or aromatherapy oils could make good audios.

Or what about interviewing a series of experts for their top tips? This works well if you know a lot of other people with expert knowledge in your field. Talk to all your dog-breeding friends to compile an audio giving advice on the best breeds for different kinds of people, for example. What are the best kinds of dogs for people with small children? Which dogs appreciate lots of exercise so make a good pet for keen hikers, ramblers or runners? Which breeds make the best guard dogs? And what's the best way to train them? Play around with ideas like this to see if you come up with something that's a good fit for you.

Courses and classes

If you're best in a hands-on helping role, what about running courses or classes? Could you run a local meditation class or a regular yoga session? What about a Saturday morning baking class or a flower-arranging course? For some of these you might need some kind of certification, but don't assume that it's necessary. It's often not essential so long as you're not awarding qualifications.

Local council regulations may stipulate that you need a Food Hygiene qualification if you are teaching cookery (and, even if you don't need it, it might be a good idea to have one!) You may also need to be covered by insurance if you're teaching any kind of fitness or movement class where people might fall or sprain muscles. But the obstacles may be fewer than you think.

Don't overlook the possibilities of creating an online course. To do this you prepare the lessons as videos, audios or written exercises which the participants pay to access. This can seem very daunting at first, but there are all kinds of course-hosting websites such as Udemy that do most of the administrative work and the marketing for you. They also usually have lots of online tutorials on how to become an instructor and how to design courses.

This isn't a book on how to make money from your expertise, so I'm trying to give you ideas, rather than detailed instructions, but there are books and online courses to teach you all the skills you need - you just have to look! Once you are clear what it is that you want to do, it becomes obvious what skills and information you'll need. The clearer you become, the easier it is to find what you want.

Products

The final category to think about is to make products. This won't be suitable for everyone, but it might work for you. Think about your expertise. Could it be turned into:

- Cosmetics or beauty products?
- Furniture?
- Greeting cards?
- Food?
- Art?
- Gifts?
- Plants or products for the garden?
- Collectors' items?

Products to avoid on the whole are clothes or toys for children - because you have to comply with lots of safety legislation. Legally, you can't sell home-

Reprogramming your Money-Mind

made alcohol without a licence, so that's not really a possibility, either. And obviously, there are a few other products that are illegal - drugs, guns and pornography spring to mind. But that still leaves a lot of options to investigate!

If you'd like a good book to read that explores in much more depth the idea of turning all kinds of expertise into money, then I'd most heartily recommend a book by John Williams called "Screw Work, Let's Play: Doing what you love and getting paid for it." Find it here, on Amazon: *http://ow.ly/UWfw1*

Reading this book 5 years ago helped me launch myself into self-employment, doing what I love. I also did John's online 30-day Challenge programme, which was the most tremendous fun! Imagine an online community of maybe 50 or 60 people all challenged to come up with a saleable product or service within 30 days - and to report back every day on their progress. All of this while getting daily instructions and support to help us do it. Really fantastic!

You can learn more here:
http://www.screwworkletsplay.com/gofurther/
Please note, I'm not getting paid in any way for recommending John - I'm simply a satisfied customer!

Having a business "on the side"

If turning your expertise into cash seems like dauntingly hard work, there is another possibility that I'll mention here.

Network Marketing

Networking marketing is a fantastic way to learn about business in a hands-on way. The idea is that you sell someone else's products for them - and get commission on each sale. If you persuade a friend or colleague to sign up to the business, and you help to train them, you also make a small profit on all of their sales. If they then sign up another person and help to train them, you both make a profit on that person's sales.

Some people confuse this with illegal pyramid schemes, but it isn't the same thing at all. It's entirely legal and is subject to a host of regulations, making it a relatively safe way to be in business for yourself. The companies vary in the amount and quality of training they provide but most are very good.

I'm not currently a member of any network marketing organisation, so I have no personal axe to grind here, or personal recommendations to make. Obviously, you need to pick an organisation whose products you really like and can get enthusiastic about. If the thought of being excited about toothpaste seems ludicrous to you, don't pick that kind of a company. Pick a company that sells vitamins, household products or cosmetics - something that you *could* get enthusiastic about.

Almost as important as the quality of products is the quality of the person who introduces you and acts as your coach. It's really important to pick someone who is making a success of the business. If they aren't, they'll never be able to show you how to do so.

Network marketing is likely to work best for you if you're fairly extraverted, with a big social circle of friends and acquaintances. You need to know some people with a bit of get-up-and-go, who'll also get excited about the idea of running their own business. It's not impossible to succeed if you don't know anyone like that, but it's definitely much harder work.

The good thing about network marketing is that it does tend to reward you in proportion to the work you put in. And it's possible to do well simply by selling a lot of products, if the idea of recruiting and training a team is totally off-putting. But having said that, for people who are prepared to put in the work - the very real and quite intense work - on themselves and on their business - network marketing can literally be a doorway to millions.

Wendy Aridela

If you've never heard of network marketing and have no idea what I'm talking about, here are a few websites to look at. This is NOT a comprehensive list! I haven't belonged to all of these companies - but I have known people who were members and so can honestly say that they seem to be reputable.

Forever Living - aloe vera products

Arbonne - Swiss skincare and beauty products

Nature's Sunshine - Healthy Living and Eating

Usana - high-quality food supplements

Neals Yard Remedies - organic skincare products

Utility Warehouse - discounted gas, electricity, phone and broadband

Nikken - magnetic products and healthcare

Partylite- scented candles and homewares, sold through parties

Saving - Your super-highway to wealth

Do you remember where I talked about why the New Age approach of "fake it until you make it" can be such a route to disaster if you're setting out to be wealthier? So many people who come across that idea and take it to heart simply end up with a maxed-out credit card! This is because they are copying the part of being wealthy that they see wealthy people doing - spending money - without having copied all the parts they don't see - making money, investing money, and saving money. If you want to *feel* wealthy, if you want to truly *be* wealthy, saving is your super-highway.

I can't afford to save

When you don't have much money coming in, it can be easy to put the whole idea of saving onto one side. Maybe later, you may think to yourself. I'll save when I've got more money. But truly, you can't afford *not* to save. Apart from the obvious reason that saving money means you are slowly *becoming* a wealthier person, there's an astonishing and interesting psychological benefit to saving.

Just as being generous helps you to see yourself as a wealthy person - you must have plenty, because here you are, giving some of it away - saving has a similar effect. Saving is one of the key things that wealthy people do. It's one of the biggest differences between people who are comfortably-off and people who feel poor. Poor people don't save. Rich people always save. So, from the very first moment that you start saving, you are behaving like a wealthy person. And just as being generous can cause big shifts in how you think and feel about yourself, so can saving.

So why do so many people prefer to spend money rather than save it? The answer lies in the feelings you associate with spending compared with the feelings associated with spending. So let's stop and think about what those feelings might be. What are the feelings you associate with spending money? I'm not talking about buying the absolute necessities of life here - toilet rolls, bread, toothpaste and so on - but about the extras. This is money you *could* save - but are choosing to spend on a coffee, some cake, a bar of chocolate, a magazine, some extra-nice cheese, a bottle of wine ....

What are the feelings you associate with that kind of spending? Is it fun? Comfort after a difficult day? A sense of rewarding yourself for hard work? Excitement? Pleasure? Anticipation - of how nice you'll smell after you've used the new cologne or how great you'll look in the new shirt?

Now - what are the feelings you associate with saving? For many people, it's a sense of duty, a feeling of heaviness, a sense of going without. What is it for you? Fill in the table below and then we'll start thinking about how to change things.

SPENDING and SAVING

How I feel about SPENDING	How I feel about SAVING

Now, what do you notice? What's the balance of negative and positive feelings between the two columns? Which column was harder to fill in? Did you find it hard to do an exercise like this that invites you to look at what your feelings are - when you've probably never noticed before how you feel or how your feelings make you do the things you do?

You're in the majority if you found this exercise challenging. And you're also in the majority if you had more positive feelings about spending than you did about saving. If you're one of the few people who feels really good about saving and has a regular habit of saving, you can skip this next section. But if you see saving as dreary, dutiful, or as something you've never really done, so you don't have any feelings about it, the next section will help.

Feeling good about saving

In order for saving to be something you do regularly, you need to feel good about it. It can't be a duty, or a "should" and especially not a miserable "should!" So let's think about what having savings means.

Having savings means that you can feel safe. If something goes wrong, you have money to help fix it. If you - or a family member - gets sick you can get treatment, and there are no worries about taking time off work, so you can have all the time you need to be fully recovered before you return.

Having money in the bank means fewer worries. No more waking up in the night in a panic about the bills - even if they are higher than normal, you have it covered. So having savings brings you greater peace

Reprogramming your Money-Mind

of mind. Knowing that you and your family are well provided for and that you have a safety-net against most of the everyday disasters - the unexpected car-repair, the burst pipe, the spilt paint, the broken window, you can relax and enjoy life more.

And there's a real pay-off in terms of self-respect. Every penny you save tells you that you are choosing the path of wealth. You are behaving like a rich person rather than a poor person. You're not just day-dreaming about being more prosperous - you're making it happen. You're actually becoming the wealthier person that you want to be. You're not just talking about it. You're following through.

I remember the time when I wrote off my car in an accident. It was a fairly old car, so the insurance pay-out didn't cover the cost of a new one, unless I was prepared to buy myself some dreadful old banger. And then I remembered a savings account that I'd got £5000 in. I took out the money and bought myself a replacement car. It wasn't new, but it was a lot better than the car I'd written off.

This was a real turning-point for me. My father had always told me how hopeless I was with money. He'd said it so many times that I had completely accepted it as truth. I'm hopeless with money. I'm stupid with money. But it hit me with such force to realise that I wasn't *that* stupid - after all, I had just bought myself a new car from my savings!

Wendy Aridela

Not only did I get a new car - but also a new image of myself. I'm actually quite competent around money. I'm careful and prudent with money. I'm not an idiot! I'm OK. I'm OK with money. I hadn't even realised up until then that I had had a belief I was stupid with money and couldn't be trusted to look after it. I hadn't noticed how much I'd taken my father's evaluation of me so totally on-board. But that was the beginning of starting to reassess my beliefs around money and move towards seeing myself as deserving to have more.

It doesn't matter if in the beginning, you can only save £1 each week. The important thing is that you start to see yourself as someone who saves. You start to see yourself who is serious about being more prosperous, someone who is taking action on it. You start to see yourself as someone who is trustworthy around money and who can handle money well. This is such a good feeling.

And something so interesting happens as you save. At first, your savings account might look pathetic. You look at your balance and see that you have saved £25 - and wonder what all the fuss is about and why you bother. But if you continue to save, you'll reach a tipping point. It may come when you have £100 or £1000 in your savings account. For you, it may not come until you have £5000 or even £50,000 - but there will come a day when you look at your savings account and feel a warm glow. You

Reprogramming your Money-Mind

feel a sudden surge of pride in yourself. You've achieved something good. And as you begin to feel this, it gets easier and easier to save. You find more ways to do it. You find yourself less inclined to waste money on little bits and pieces of stuff you don't really need or even really want.

But also, as you come to see yourself as a genuinely wealthier person, you'll attract more money into your life. You may get a better job. Bigger, better deals may come your way. Doors open. New opportunities pop up all over the place. The energy you are putting out into the world has changed. You're putting out the energy of being wealthy - and so that's what is coming back to you.

Making saving more rewarding

Have you ever saved up some money - and then taken it all out of your account because of an unexpected bill? Or Christmas/Hanukah/Eid? Me too! So how can you build up a body of saved money that you're not constantly tempted to break into? The secret is to have more than one savings account.

I first came across this idea in a Nightingale Conant audio programme called Prosperity Consciousness by Fredric Lehrman - which you can find here: *http://www.nightingale.com/prosperity-consciousness.html* Since then, I've come across variations of it in several books and audio programmes. It works best, I think, if you customise it to fit your own needs, rather than following a formula that someone else designed to suit them.

But the basic idea is very simple - you have different savings accounts, with different rules attached to each one. You can have as many accounts as you like. Although banks are generally not keen on you having lots of different current/checking accounts, they're usually open to the idea of you having several savings accounts. To begin with, it's maybe worth starting with just two - a long-term savings account to build your financial freedom with, and one other. Once you're in the habit of saving, you can add more, to suit yourself. So, what are the different accounts you could have, and what are the rules associated with each one?

Savings Accounts - which ones would feel best for you?

The biggest mistake that many people make is to have just one savings account. The trouble with this is that you're trying to achieve conflicting goals with it. Are you saving for a holiday or saving for a new dishwasher? It's easier to keep savings separate so that your rules - and your goals - are always clear. You may think of others, but here are some ideas to get you started:

- ***Financial Freedom Account*** - the point of this account is to build up savings to the point

Reprogramming your Money-Mind

where you could give up work if you chose to, and could retire comfortably. Even if you love your job, this is a good savings account to have in place. The time may come in the future when you feel you'd like to stop working and do something else, and this account gives you the freedom to do that.

The rule is simple - pay money in and never, ever take it out, except to invest it in financial products that will bring you a greater return. I'm not a financial professional of any kind, so I'm leaving it as open-ended as that. You need to talk to a financial advisor once you have enough money in this account to make it worthwhile to do so, and draw up a plan with them about where best to place it, in order to get you the specific outcome you want , whether that's a pension fund or something else.

- *Free-from-Debt account* - the idea of this account is to pay off any debts more quickly and to get you debt-free as fast as possible. The rule is that you only take money from this account to pay off debts.

  A sensible strategy is to use this to pay off first the debts which have the highest rates of interest, as generally, that's going to make the most difference. But, as I said before, I'm not a financial professional so take advice on which

debts it's best to pay off first if the answer isn't blindingly obvious.
- **The Fun-and-Frolics Account** - the point of this is to stop you being tempted to take the money out of your other savings accounts by having one whose whole purpose is for you to have fun. The rule for this account is that you can only spend it on having fun!
It's up to you whether that's a big thing, like a trip round the world or a smaller thing like a concert ticket or a cream tea at the Ritz. But save it until there's enough to buy something you wouldn't normally think you can afford - something that's a real treat. This is a tremendous incentive to save because it gives you regular experiences of living a wealthier lifestyle. You don't just get to see your favourite band perform - you have a VIP ticket, right in front of the stage. Or you have a holiday on another continent. Or you buy a designer suit. It's totally up to you!
- **Big Purchases Account** - the point of this is to save for a new car, new windows for your home, or whatever else you would like. It allows you to either pay the whole amount in cash - which often gets you a substantial discount - or to pay a much bigger deposit/initial payment and so to have considerably lower monthly payments.

Reprogramming your Money-Mind

> The rule for this is to save up until you have enough money for what you want - whether that's the whole cash price of the item or a larger-than-usual deposit. If you want more than one large purchase, you may prefer to have several accounts. In this way, you can withdraw the money for the new dishwasher without feeling you've just spent the money for the new car.
>
> - ***The Safety-Net account*** - the point of this is to cover the worst of life's emergencies. If your roof gets blown off in a freak storm, or your child gets a couple of teeth knocked out and needs implants, this is your contingencies fund. The rule is to pay money in and only withdraw it in an emergency.

Now you have the idea, keep it in the back of your mind for a day or two. What do you *need to* save for? What would you *like to* save for? Now, what are your priorities? If you could only start one account this month, which one would it be? What would be your second choice? Open those two first-choice accounts this month. It doesn't matter if you can only put £1 into each account to begin with. The trick is always - begin. You can build from there!

The joy of this is that your savings *mean* something. You're not just putting money into the bank. You're taking one more small step towards the home of your dreams, the holiday-of-a-lifetime or the new car

193

you've been wanting. You can see for yourself that every month is bringing your dreams that bit closer. You're doing it! You're making it real! And that is the behaviour of truly wealthy people.

One useful tip for saving more is to keep a spare-change purse in your pocket, bag or car. Whenever you get given a load of coppers, put them straight into the spare-change purse - they're inconvenient to carry round, anyway.

Then, in addition, every time you are tempted to buy yourself a little treat - a bar of chocolate or a latte, perhaps, give yourself a choice. Do you want to spend the money or put it in the spare-change purse? You were going to spend it on something non-essential, so clearly you can afford to do without it. At the end of every week, pay in the money from your spare-change purse into one or other of your savings accounts.

You can leave it longer and pay it in once a month, if you are embarrassed to pay in tiny amounts of money each week - but the longer you keep it hanging about, the greater is the temptation to spend it! Once you get into a regular habit of saving, and you can trust yourself to save that money, come what may, you can let it accumulate to more respectable amounts. But initially, I found the idea of saving each week a useful discipline.

Investing - creating a better world for your children

I used to think that investing was some arcane activity carried out by men in top hats. It wasn't something ordinary people would ever do. (I told you my family had some odd beliefs about money, didn't I?) But once you start to build up money in a long-term savings account, sooner or later, you're going to start thinking about investing. Most longer-term savings plans are based on investment in the stock market.

And even if you don't want to think about any of that and just want to keep your money in the bank, sooner or later, you start to be aware of what the banks do with the money people such as yourself are giving them to manage. They are investing it. Do you know what your bank is investing *your* money in? Some banks have a clear policy of ethical investing, but with other banks, the priority is making the maximum amount of money - so they may be investing in things that you, personally, would rather not do. And they are using your money to do it.

What you are doing with your money when you invest it is that you are helping to bring about the kind of world you'd like your children to live in. You're putting your money where your values are. So, obviously, if you'd like your children to grow up in a peaceful world, free of war, you may not want to invest in weapons manufacturers. And if you wanted them to grow up in a world full of healthy people, you'd probably not want to invest in tobacco companies. To me, that's a no-brainer. So, at some stage, you may want to take a closer look at the ethical investment priorities of your bank.

What kind of world do you want?

If you want to be a wealthier person, you have to get used to the idea that where you spend your money and where you save your money makes a difference in the world. Money confers the power to make a difference. More money means you have more power. It may not make an enormous difference at this point - but lots of small differences add up. So you want to develop an awareness of what are the long-term effects of your spending and your saving.

Do you want to live in a world where every High Street is the same, full of the same supermarkets and chain-stores? Or do you prefer a world where small businesses thrive and every town sells different things, depending on the skills and talents of local people, what the local industries are and what kinds of crops grow well in the local area? There isn't one right answer. There are pros and cons. But every time you spend your money you are, in effect, voting for one kind of High Street over the other.

Reprogramming your Money-Mind

Do you want your children to grow up in a world where they can walk in the woods, explore the wilderness, swim in the sea, and find wild animals and plants in rich abundance all around? Or don't you think it matters? You keep voting with your wallet, whether you think about it or not. Even before you have the wealth you want, start to think like a wealthier person. Realise that even though you may not yet have a share portfolio, you are investing in the future all the time. What kind of a world are you bringing about?

Wendy Aridela

Set Yourself Up for Success!

As I've been saying all the way through this book, your Money-Programming is multi-layered. What you earn, spend and save is tied up with your beliefs about money and success, how you feel about yourself and what you see as your life-purpose. So although the common-sense first step to having more money might seem to be to just get a better paid job, sometimes the solution, or part of the solution, is less obvious. So let's have a look at some of the more alternative approaches that could turn out to make a much bigger difference than you expect.

Clutter-clearing - making way for new opportunities

In the last decade, interest in the Chinese art of Feng Shui has really taken off. At first glance, it seems to be based on superstition - surely, it can't make that much difference what colour I paint my living-room, whether my table is round or square or where I put my television? But, whether or not you get into the detail, in its broadest sense, Feng Shui turns out to be based on good psychology.

Whether or not you accept that your world *reflects* you, it's common sense that it *affects* you. It's difficult to feel abundant and prosperous if your home is dirty, shabby, untidy and cluttered. It's

Reprogramming your Money-Mind

harder to have faith in yourself as a loveable person if your living room is full of furniture your ex-partner bought, so that even sitting on your sofa brings him or her to mind - along with memories of the awful things that happened between you that led to the break-up. It's as if your furniture carries bad memories and associations. So have a look around you and start thinking about the small changes you could make that would set you up for success.

You don't have to study the mysteries of Feng Shui to guess that if half the drawers in your filing cabinet are full of old paperwork you haven't looked at in years, the energy that they are putting out into your home or your workplace isn't going to be positive. Similarly, you don't need to be a Feng Shui Grand Master to understand that if you can't even get a saucepan out of your kitchen cupboard without collapsing a pile of utensils, you'd feel less stressed around food and cooking once you'd reorganised things.

This may seem like a lot of woo-woo purple bean-sprouts until you try it. And then, you realise that, heck, clearing out just that one drawer has made a real difference to how the room feels. Or that clearing out your wardrobe or your kitchen cabinet has made *you* feel better, even if the house feels no different! And it won't be long, once you get seriously into de-cluttering before you start to hit the "Feng Shui Magic."

Wendy Aridela

The Feng Shui 'Magic'

It's silly. It has to be a coincidence. Logically, there can't be a connection. (Can there?) But, wow! It just so happened that, right after you'd taken the plunge and thrown out your ex-partner's sofa, you meet Ms or Mr Wonderful and begin a new relationship. It seems as if throwing away the last remnants of the old one has somehow made some space for a new one. Now, whether that space is in your living-room, in your house or in your head, who knows? But here is this wonderful new lover and hey, who cares?

Or you clear out that filing cabinet - at long last! - and within a week, some totally unexpected business opportunity pops up. Again, it seems that by creating some space, you've made room for something new to come into your life. Talk to anyone who's tried it - don't take my word for it. Ask colleagues at work or look online. There are simply hundreds, if not thousands of stories like this.

Whether or not you believe that clutter is a way of hoarding stale, dead, energy in your house that keeps your good from coming to you, it stands to reason that living clutter free is more efficient and so frees up energy for something else - such as meeting Ms or Mr Wonderful. Or, indeed, coming up with the Million-Dollar Idea that turns your life around.

So, take a look around you and pick a little project that you could get started on. Then make a commitment to yourself that you'll have it done by next weekend. And then do it! Who knows what you might be making room for?

Letting go of the past

Whenever you're setting out to have a changed life - to be a somewhat different version of yourself than you have ever been before, it's useful to take real, physical action to prove to your subconscious mind that things are different now. Clutter-clearing is a powerful form of this. Perhaps even more powerful is to move house - and it's amazing how often the opportunity to do that will crop up once you start to make changes.

If moving home isn't possible, or desirable, decorating often is. In fact, now, I tend to see any desire in myself to decorate - especially if I seem to want to take on half the house - as evidence that I'm brewing up for changes. I don't know what it is about colour, but the colours in my home do really seem to reflect my life. One of the signs that I'm changing is that I want different colours around me.

I can have a pink bedroom for years and then suddenly wake up one day and hate it. It's obvious to me that I'd be much happier in a blue bedroom or a green one. Or I can feel comfortable in my living room until one day, all of a sudden, I see it as shabby and want to repaint it. I've found by experience that these wild desires to recolour my home seem to go hand-in-hand with desires to reshape my life.

So, how are you going to reflect your new identity as a wealthy person back to yourself? What changes will you make? Remember - your environment always reflects your deepest beliefs about who you really are.

Your appearance

I find it interesting to look at my friends and acquaintances and to notice who seems to be going through big changes. Sooner or later, that person will change their appearance. They may gain weight, lose weight, start to dye their hair, stop dyeing their hair, or dye their hair a different colour. They may start to dress more smartly or to wear more comfortable, casual clothes. They may change the colours they wear. With some, the changes are small and subtle, while with others, they are enormous - the person no longer looks like their old self at all.

If you've gone through a big shift in your wealth-identity don't be surprised if you feel a deep urge to change your appearance, too. I'm not talking here about dressing for success in any conventional sense, unless that's really what you feel drawn to do.

I'm talking about changing your appearance to match your new sense of who you are. You may start by buying one item of clothing in a colour you've almost never worn before. Or you may get your hair re-styled. Allow yourself some time to feel you way forward. It can be tempting to simply book yourself in with an image consultant and have a style-and-colour analysis - and that can be a wonderfully empowering thing to do. But my advice would be to hold off until you have at least a rough idea of who you are, in this new, updated, wealthier version.

Are you now drawn to being a much sharper dresser, to having a more crisp and smart appearance? Or have you spent years wearing drab, stiff suits to work and find that you now want to wear softer, more casual and more colourful clothes? Would you like to wear more jewellery? Do you want to have one or two key items of designer clothes, even if that means saving for them? Or do you feel wealthier in something very quiet and under-stated, but of excellent quality, or made in luxurious materials?

There isn't a right answer. But what you'll find is that dressing in a way that makes you feel wealthier works wonders. You start to see yourself differently - and so do other people. You become visible to all kinds of people who wouldn't have noticed you before. New doors open. New opportunities arise. So have fun with your exploration!

Wendy Aridela

Don't stop with your clothes - change your body, too!

As I said in some of the previous sections, abundance is a two-way street. The wealth you have coming in is a reflection of the energy you are putting out. So it makes sense to open the floodgates of your energy as wide as possible.

The more high-powered, dynamic, radiant, energised and healthy you can make your physical body, the more you become someone other people want to be around. The healthier your body is, the more clearly you'll find yourself thinking. You'll have the creative and dynamic energy to do more, create more, sell more, inspire more, make a bigger difference - or whatever it's important to you to put your energy into. You'll spend more of your working day being productive rather than slumped in a grey mess of brain-fog and exhaustion.

In short, you'll be more valuable - which will tend to bring more money, opportunities, job-satisfaction, respect, thanks - abundance in many forms - flowing back into your life.

So how can you achieve this? Well, I'm not a fitness coach, a doctor or a dietician, so I'm only going to talk in the most general terms here. Do get some expert help if you feel you want to make big changes and you want a personalised fitness or wellbeing plan for yourself.

Reprogramming your Money-Mind

But I do have some simple, common-sense advice. Keeping a food diary is an unexpectedly powerful thing to do, for example. For a week, write down every single thing that you eat or drink, honestly. Every hour or two, make a note of how you are feeling. Are you energised and clear-thinking? Or have you suddenly gone foggy, sleepy, irritable, or anxious? Are you aching anywhere? Do you have a headache? Keep this up for 7 days.

Now comes the interesting bit. Find all the places where your energy suddenly slumped - you went shaky, sleepy, foggy, irritable or just dull and apathetic. Notice what you ate or drank in the two hours beforehand, each time. Do you spot any patterns? If not, see if these energy slumps correspond to something you ate or drank the previous day.

Some food intolerances show a delayed effect. For example, if I drink milk, I feel fine for the rest of the day. But the following day, my "bad back" plays up and I get arthritic pains in my hands. In my 50s, I thought I was inheriting the arthritis that my mother, grandmother and great-grandmother had, to varying degrees. Bad luck, I thought. Still, that's genetics for you - it's clearly a strong family pattern. Then I kept a food diary - and noticed how the joint pain seemed to follow drinking milk and eating cheese. I tried a dairy-free diet and found it made a fantastic difference - I'm almost completely free of pain or discomfort in my joints, unless I accidentally eat or drink something with milk in it. So be aware of delayed effects.

What you're mainly looking for here are foods that sap your energy and dim your light. Experiment! Try making a few tweaks to your diet and noting the effects. I don't know what you'll find because people are so different.

Your energy-zappers may be totally different from mine. I feel better if I don't eat bread. You may thrive on bread but notice that potatoes or cheese make you feel sleepy or foggy. I know someone who gets a headache if they eat or drink anything that contains the artificial sweetener aspartame - yet can cheerily consume lots of sugar. Other people notice that they feel more irritable the more sugar they consume - but aspartame doesn't seem to affect them. In the end, the real expert on your body is going to be you.

Once you have identified your energy-zappers, you want to discover which foods make you feel good. Which are the foods that give you the most energy? Can you discover a way of eating that seems to give you maximum clarity of thought? There are many different ways to eat, some of which work well for some people and not for others. Some possibilities for you to investigate might include:

- The Paleo way of eating

Reprogramming your Money-Mind

- The alkaline foods way of eating
- The Mediterranean way of eating
- the Ayurvedic way of eating

There are others. But all of these are fairly healthy ways of eating, based on whole foods and lots of fruits and vegetables, so they are good places to start.

This isn't a short-term project . It may take you a year or so - or even longer than that - to discover how to feel at your best all of the time. But it's very worthwhile. By tuning into your own body and noticing how it responds to what you eat and drink you can end up with better energy than you have ever had, whatever your age.

The last few sections may seem to have very little to do with money - yet you might find that the changes I suggest have completely unexpected knock-on effects on your finances. You can probably tell as you read whether or not a particular idea is worth trying. When I first read about clutter-clearing, for example, it instantly rang bells in my head. And anytime my life feels stuck, I know I can get things moving again by sorting through some cupboards or by giving away a bunch of my unwanted clothes or books to a charity shop.

But if you read about repainting your living-room and it just leaves you feeling flat, don't do it! If the

Wendy Aridela

idea of sorting through your wardrobe feels like the dreariest possible way to spend a wet weekend afternoon, skip that suggestion. But there *is* a power in changing your environment to reflect the new you, however you do that. Experiment until you find a way to do it for you.

Finding the way through

The 'Richard Branson' exercise

Some of you may be feeling a sense of complete overwhelm as you read through this section. "This is all well and good," you may think, "but what about *my* life? *My* life is a mess. I have all these special circumstances that make me an exception to everything you've said. There are all kinds of reasons why this would never work for *me*. So what can *I* do?" Well, I have a suggestion. Try the 'Richard Branson' exercise.

Imagine what would happen if one morning, Richard Branson woke up as you. He would still know everything that he knows about running a business and having a great deal of fun in the process, but he'd be living your life. He'd only have your money and your income to start with and he'd only know the people that you now know.

Remember that you're thinking about one of the most brilliant business people of this century, someone who seems able to make a success of just about anything. There's no way that your life would utterly stump him. He'd enjoy the challenge of thinking of a way to turn things round. So what do you imagine he would do?

What do you think his first steps might be? How long do you think it would take him to double your income? Do you think he could end up earning five or ten times what you earn? How long do you think that might take? What other changes do you think he might make? What kinds of people would he take steps to network with? What kind of a business do you think he'd set about creating, with your life as a starting point?

Now, let these ideas fizz around your brain for a bit, sparking off all kinds of inspiration. Which of those 'Richard Branson' steps could *you* take? What new ideas has this exercise sparked?

If you found yourself thinking that he could do miraculous things with your life because he knows how to do XYZ, which you don't know how to do, what could you do to learn it? Whatever you think XYZ is - marketing, networking, or hot-air ballooning - if you see that as the skill that makes the difference, what could you do about that?

If you thought that he would succeed because he has a different kind of personality from you, what do you think are the traits that make the difference? Could you develop more of those traits in yourself? Could you be more fun-loving, more courageous or more visionary? What would have to change?

If you feel you are too different to even take steps towards being more like Richard Branson, is there a successful business person you feel more in resonance with? Is Sir Alan Sugar more your type, for example? Which of the Dragon's Den judges do you feel most akin to? Now try this exercise again, using them, instead of Sir Richard Branson.

This exercise may not give you the one-step magical path out of the muddle, but hopefully, it may spark some ideas. At the very least, it imprints in your subconscious that there is a path - and probably more than one path - that leads through to the other side of the difficult patch you are in right now.

Getting help

You are not alone. And however muddled and messy your finances or your life might be, there are people who can help you. Don't be too proud to ask. One of the characteristics of very wealthy people is that they know their own strengths and weaknesses and they never try to act alone from an area of weakness.

They may have accountants to do their books for them, marketing managers to do the publicity and advertising for their businesses and personal trainers to keep them fit. They might have a cook to prepare their food, a housekeeper to do the cleaning and the laundry and a personal assistant to answer emails and organise their appointment diary. They don't try to do everything themselves.

So, if you decide to seek help, you're behaving like a wealthy and powerful person - it's weak, insecure and desperate people who bury their heads in the sand who refuse to ask for help and hope that all these nasty problems will go away. They won't. Who can help? Well, that depends what your needs and problems are. But here are some ideas:

- Book-keepers
- Accountants
- Financial advisors
- Debt-management services/charities
- Local colleges - for courses on money-management, plus practical skills such as book-keeping or running a small business
- Online courses - good for specific technical skills such as video making, social media marketing, and using software well
- Network marketing organisations - to learn skills to run a small business
- Business networking groups - for making useful contacts and becoming more confident in talking about your business
- Toastmasters - to develop your public speaking skills
- Life coaches/business coaches - for skilled one-on-one help in making changes to your life or your business
- Bookshops - you can find books that will teach you almost anything!
- YouTube - again, you can find videos that will teach you almost anything!

Reprogramming your Money-Mind

- Diet coaches/nutritionists - to help you develop a personal wellbeing plan
- Image consultants - to work with you on changing your appearance to reflect the new you.
- Man-with-a-van/ clutter-clearing specialists - can help if you've been a hoarder for years and now want a massive clear-out.

As the saying goes, the only people who *enjoy* change are babies with wet nappies! Getting the support and help you need can make the whole process easier.

Wendy Aridela

Conclusion
How will your life be different now?

CONCLUSION: what are the changes you want to see?

What would it be like, having Money-Programming that worked *for* you, instead of against you? What are the changes you want to see?

Most of us spend most of our waking moments at work. So it should be one of the greatest sources of joy in our lives. Yet I see far too many people for whom work is a grind, a dull drudgery, a frantic daily frustration, even something of a nightmare. I see people with amazing gifts and talents who keep them bottled up, or shut into a tiny corner of their life - because they feel trapped by the need to work for money at something that keeps them small, grey and dull.

For myself, I would love to see a world where every single person earns their living doing something they love, something that makes their heart sing. I passionately believe that this is a world with no spare parts - that every single person on the planet is uniquely gifted and talented. Every single person holds part of the solution to the world's problems. Everyone has a contribution to make. Each one of us is a vital part of the whole.

I'd love to see a world where we're all sane around money. A world where we work at what we love, for the amount of time each week that feels balanced and fulfilling - in return for an income that lets us live a rich life.

A rich life includes money, but it also includes warm and loving connections with people we care about, time to appreciate our children growing, time for leisure, rest and simple enjoyment, and the satisfaction that comes from making a difference - in our family, in our community, in the world. A rich life is one where we live in harmony with Nature, rather than in opposition to it. It's a world full of beauty, both natural and man-made. It's a world in which all people count.

A rich life is one in which we all have abundance on every level - physical comfort and security, peace with ourselves, our neighbours and our world, health and wellbeing on every level and a life filled with joy and laughter. Getting sane around money is a part of that - neither running after money as the ultimate good nor disparaging it as the evil mechanism of exploitation and greed.

This is clearly an ideal, maybe even a 'castle in the air.' But as Henry Thoreau famously wrote:
"If you have built castles in the air, your work need not be lost; that is where they should be. Now put the foundations under them."

Ideal worlds happen as one person after another takes hold of the ideal and starts to live it. My dream in life is to help more and more people to do the work that makes their heart sing, the work that lets them make the difference to the world they feel drawn to make. Money-Programming is what so often gets in the way of that - and that's why I wrote this book. If this helps even a few people to move towards a life where they feel able to shine their light more brightly and sing the song of their heart loudly enough for more people to hear it, I shall be well pleased.

Extra Bits
My Story and more

EXTRA BITS

My Story

Meet Wendy Aridela

I've been meditating for more than 40 years and have been on a spiritual path for even longer. This has many good points - feeling happy and living a very rich life being two of them. But I've had to travel a long way to get here.

My family was just about as dysfunctional as possible where money was concerned - including a "Black Sheep" uncle suspected of money-laundering for the Mafia. (You don't get a lot more dysfunctional than that!)

My paternal grandparents had been young during the Great Depression of the 1930s and had powerful and bitter memories of having to stand in queues at a soup-kitchen when my Grandfather was laid off from work. Meanwhile, my maternal grandparents had had a series of grocery stores, where the profits were increased by my Grandfather's less-than-totally-honest business practices. These were always talked about as evidence of how clever he was, but even by my teenage years, I knew enough to realise that many of them were dishonest and some of them were downright illegal.

Wendy Aridela

Both my parents had grown up during the war-times years so their lives had been shaped by rationing and the tremendous poverty-consciousness that arose from a decade or more of make-do-and-mend.

My mother responded to all of this by adding up every penny, keeping lists of outgoings and repeatedly telling us that we couldn't afford this or that. I remember the guilt I felt for continuing to grow when she complained that she'd had the same Winter coat for 10 years and couldn't afford another because we children kept growing and so constantly needing new clothes and shoes. From her, I picked up a whole lot of fears around money - including the constant fear that it would run out entirely. I also ended up with a feeling that I didn't deserve to have money spent on me.

My father, on the other hand, was determined to escape from the poverty of his childhood. During his period of National Service he had mixed with people from much wealthier backgrounds and had seen that what he had previously thought of as unbelievable luxury was what they considered as normal. He wanted the kind of lifestyle he imagined them having. So he bought a constant stream of expensive treats - luxury chocolates, cutting-edge gadgets, and music LPs. However, much of this was funded by debt and eventually culminated in bankruptcy.

Reprogramming your Money-Mind

He had some very odd beliefs around money - I remember him explaining to me that the only people who could ever be rich were those who were either born into the aristocracy or criminals. He felt that how much money someone had determined their worth as a person to a large degree, so that even if you were clever and talented, or well-loved and kind, it was all a bit of a waste of time unless it made you rich and preferably famous, too.

As a constant back-drop to all of this, we were brought up as strict Roman Catholics. There was a clear understanding in our family, therefore, that poverty was more spiritual than wealth and that rich people were likely to go to Hell, en masse. This "spiritual" idea that money was intrinsically bad was compounded when I left home and moved into an ashram.

Living in an ashram in the 1970s taught that money was profoundly unspiritual and that as this world was illusory, anyway, material interests were best avoided. Not a useful attitude once you leave the ashram and have children to care for! The combination of a bunch of unhelpful "spiritual" beliefs around money and success plus the astonishingly unhelpful pile of "male-cow manure" that resulted from my upbringing meant my learning curve around money, success and valuing my own gifts and talents has been steep.

Wendy Aridela

From an early age, I had a strong sense of wanting to be some kind of helper or healer. My original plan was to be an Educational Psychologist but as (by then) a single parent with three children, I couldn't afford to do the training. However, I found a way to do something with the same kind of feel to it by becoming a specialist teacher for children with behavioural and learning difficulties. Because I was a specialist, the pay was good and I spent years at the top of the teaching salary scale. However, the call to be doing something different grew and grew until it reached a point where I was faced with a choice - keep the secure job or do something new?..........

It would be nice to be able to say that I made the choice with the obvious spiritual Brownie points attached. Everyone who has ever read any spiritual development/ follow your destiny type of books knows very well that the "right" answer at this point is to follow your heart and trust Spirit to make it all work out, right?

Yes, well, that's the benefit of hindsight for you! I chose the other path - I went for a more specialised, more highly paid teaching job that I thought would bring me more status and more job satisfaction - and would hopefully settle that niggling sense that I should be moving on and doing something else with my life. Boy, oh boy, what a mistake! Did you ever do something like that? - ignore what you feel the Universe was whispering in your ear? If you did, you probably experienced something similar to what happened to me - if you ignore the Universe's whispers, it starts shouting!

The job was a disaster! Suffice it to say, that when they decided to reorganise the school a couple of years down the line, and they wanted two teachers to take voluntary redundancy, I couldn't wait! The idea that they'd pay me to leave was astonishing! I discovered I was also eligible to take early retirement and to cash in my pension, so I left teaching and went into self-employment, using the healing and helping skills I'd spent 25 years developing but never really having the confidence to use, other than around the edges of my life.

And that's when the serious work on my issues around money and my own value really took off. It took me a while to see how all my skills and talents could fit together. It was only after I'd helped a lot of people turn their expertise into money - by writing books, creating courses or through developing educational games that I began to see where I could help people most to make a bigger difference.

So now, that's the focus of my work. I offer a mix-and-match range of resources to help you make more money from your expertise. Browse the website to learn more! You can find my website at: http://wendyaridela.co.uk

Wendy Aridela

FREE REPORT – THE 7 Mistakes that shut the door to Abundance

You live in an abundant world. You are gifted and talented in a unique way. You have a contribution to make to the world that nobody else can make.
And yet........Somehow, it never seems to come together in the way you feel it could.

You have wonderful skills - but no clients. Or you have wonderful clients - but no money. Or you feel stuck in a job that doesn't really express you. Maybe you feel like a "Half-time Hero" - only able to use your brilliance around the edges of life.

However it happens ..... somehow, all that Infinite Flow of Wonderfulness seems to only come your way in trickles and dribbles. So what's happening?
How are you blocking your own good?
How are you - somehow- sabotaging your own success?
Find out with my *free* Report – the 7 Mistakes that shut the door to Abundance.
You can't change anything you're not aware of!
But even noticing - and changing - one small thing can be life-changing.
If you'd like to begin your more abundant life right now, copy this link.
http://wendyaridela.co.uk

More Books by Wendy Aridela

You may also be interested in some of Wendy's other books.

Living at the Crossroads

Many people at this time are finding themselves at a crossroads in life - the way they have been living and working no longer seems to be working for them. Old roles are no longer satisfying and it feels as if they have grown out of their old identity. They are drawn to take their life in a new direction, often with no clear idea of how that will look.

These people have a strong inner sense that, somehow, they could be living more authentically and expressing more of the potential they feel deep within themselves. They know that they could be making a bigger difference in the world even if, right now, they aren't sure what that is. If this describes you, then this could be the book you have been looking for!

This is the book for everyone who is feeling the call to be more, do more, make a bigger difference and help more people. It is likely to be particularly helpful to people who feel the need to change at mid-life. Drawing on more than 40 years' experience on her own spiritual journey, Wendy offers a wealth of helpful information, inspiring new ways of looking at your life, meditation techniques and practical self-help tips to help you close the gap between who you are now, and the more radiant and inspirational self you feel drawn to become.

Find "Living at the Crossroads" here: *http://ow.ly/VcCP6*

The Goddesses of Abundance

This book introduces the Goddesses of Abundance pack of oracle cards. It includes a link for you to download the pack so that you can get started straight away exploring your relationship with Abundance. Simply print the cards onto some stiff paper or card, laminate them if you like, and you're away! There's also a black-and-white version of the cards printed at the back of the book, for you to cut out and use.

It's dedicated to every single one of you who has ever felt trapped by money. It's for everyone who has ever felt, "I'd love to earn my living doing that - but I'd never make money at it." It's for you if you long to travel, to learn new skills, to meet new people, to live the completely different life you just know you have in you - but truly believe that you can't, because of money. My prayer is that this book helps you see the possibilities with new eyes. Find "The Goddesses of Abundance" here: *http://ow.ly/VcD9G*

How to Meditate

A simple explanation of what meditation is and how to do it, written in a jargon-free style. This book makes no assumptions about your spiritual beliefs or even that you have any.

It doesn't matter if you are Christian, Buddhist, Moslem, Hindu or some other faith tradition – you will not find anything here to clash with or contradict your faith. This book is also suitable for people who would describe themselves as spiritual but not religious, seeking for a path, agnostic – or even atheist, as this book does not presume a belief in God.

Instead of you hamster-wheeling away on your mental treadmill, meditation lets you step off and smell the roses. Or taste the coffee. Or feel the texture of the pavement under your feet. Life becomes a richer experience. You see, hear and touch more. You notice the things you didn't expect – the little yellow flower growing through a crack in the pavement, the sound of the birds singing behind the noise of the traffic, the warm, cinnamon smell as you walk past the bakers.

Just sitting quietly, you discover that simply breathing can be pleasurable. You notice the cool stream of air entering your nose and then leaving again. You start to enjoy the sensations as your muscles relax. Slowly, behind all the thought-chatter, behind all the everyday noise, you become aware of a stillness and a silence that is always in the background. As you begin to relax, you realise how tense you've been all day and you can let go. You can enjoy just being with yourself for a while without the cast of thousands in your head.

Instead of allowing your mind to drag you wherever it wants to, you take back control. It's your mind, after all! You choose to focus on what's real, rather than on what's imaginary. In that way, meditation is almost the opposite of being in a trance. In fact, it's breaking the trance that most of us live in.

Find "How to Meditate" here:
http://ow.ly/VcDOa

Printed in Great Britain
by Amazon